Trapped in a Maze

Trapped in a Maze

How Social Control Institutions
Drive Family Poverty and Inequality

Leslie Paik

UNIVERSITY OF CALIFORNIA PRESS

University of California Press
Oakland, California

© 2021 by Leslie Paik

Library of Congress Cataloging-in-Publication Data

Names: Paik, Leslie, author.
Title: Trapped in a maze : how social control institutions drive family
    poverty and inequality / Leslie Paik.
Description: Oakland, California : University of California Press,
    [2021] | Includes bibliographical references and index
Identifiers: LCCN 2021006518 (print) | LCCN 2021006519 (ebook) |
    ISBN 9780520344631 (cloth) | ISBN 9780520344648 (paperback) |
    ISBN 9780520975590 (epub)
Subjects: LCSH: Poverty—Government policy—United States. | Poor
    families—United States—Social conditions. | Public welfare—United
    States.
Classification: LCC HC110.P6 P35 2021 (print) | LCC HC110.P6 (ebook) |
    DDC 362.5/5610973—dc23
LC record available at https://lccn.loc.gov/2021006518
LC ebook record available at https://lccn.loc.gov/2021006519

Manufactured in the United States of America

30 29 28 27 26 25 24 23 22 21
10 9 8 7 6 5 4 3 2 1

In honor of my mother, In Chun Paik, whose life epitomized love, faith, determination, strength, and commitment to family

Contents

Acknowledgments

Ethnographies are never conducted in solitude. This book is the result of so many people supporting me over the years. First and foremost, thank you to the families in the study who opened up their homes and shared their lives with me. This book would not have been possible without your honesty, precious time, and trust. I also want to thank the agencies who helped me recruit these families, as well as my research assistants who helped with the data collection and coding: Kyla Bender-Baird, José Cáceres, Catherine Casado-Pabon, Lori-Ann Chung, Jerry Rebollar, and Imani Richards.

To my intellectual family: Bob Emerson—you've taught me everything I know about ethnography; I am forever grateful to your continued support and mentorship. Annette Lareau, Mitch Duneier, Laurie Krivo, and Judith Levine—your feedback at the late stages of the writing was so instrumental to helping me push this project over the finish line. To my fellow scholars in the Racial Democracy, Crime and Justice Network, I am humbled to be part of this intellectual community and am so inspired by your prolific and innovative research on race and the justice system.

I want to give a special thanks to Annette Lareau for her long-standing support of this project. She graciously agreed to a lunch meeting while I was in the early stages of data collection, even though she didn't know me at all. Since that fateful meeting, she has encouraged me to carry on despite the many struggles of doing this kind of fieldwork and has challenged me to think about my data in new ways. I only hope I can inspire future generations of scholars as you have done for me and for countless others.

The National Science Foundation, Professional Staff Congress–City University of New York (CUNY), CUNY Advanced Research Collective and CUNY Office of Research provided much needed financial support and course release time for me to do the data collection and write the book. Thank you also to the anonymous reviewers at UC Press for their insightful comments on earlier drafts of the manuscript. Finally, I am so grateful to my editor, Maura Roessner, at UC Press who was enthusiastic about this project from its early stages to its final stage; I deeply appreciate for your support, patience, and feedback along the way.

On a personal note, I'd like to thank my family, especially my parents for providing my siblings and me with a strong foundation based on love, sacrifice, and financial security from which to embark on our own adventures in life. It is their commitment to our family that inspires me to do this work, to understand better the structural challenges for and efforts of other parents seeking to do the same for their children. To my friends who have become my family—Alexes Harris and L'Heureux Lewis-McCoy— thank you for keeping me grounded during this roller coaster of a project, for reading so many drafts of this work, and most importantly, for being such giving and committed friends who are always there to listen, motivate, and encourage.

I dedicate this book to the families in my study—and countless others—who love fiercely and fight tirelessly for their children, persevering in the midst of institutional racism, discrimination, and societal apathy. I hope I have done some justice to their lives in shedding light on and giving voice to struggles that we often ignore and discount.

Prologue

The Hernandez Family

The Hernandezes are a close-knit Latinx family struggling to make ends meet in New York City.[1] Seven family members from three generations live together in a cramped three-bedroom, one-bathroom apartment just off a main thoroughfare in the Bronx. The apartment is in the grandparents' names: Sandra and Eladio Hernandez. Sandra works full-time as a home health aide, and Eladio used to work in book and printmaking. They live with their two children, José and forty-five-year-old Sulia, and three of Sulia's children, Gigi, Aracely, and Isaiah. Sulia and her children share one room, while José has his own room and Sandra and Eladio share the third bedroom. Sulia's twenty-five-year-old daughter Katy, who recently moved to her boyfriend's mother's house an hour outside of the city, comes back and forth to stay, as she goes to a hospital in New York City for prenatal and neonatal care for her baby, who has to be in an incubator due to breathing problems.

This book is about the journeys that the Hernandezes and other poor families take in accessing services from a plethora of institutions to address their needs, while also getting caught up in multiple bureaucratic processes. The Hernandez family is currently dealing with seven institutions: Family Court, public assistance, Medicaid, hospitals, mental health, Supplemental Security Income (SSI), and schools. Sulia has gone to Family Court to try to get child support from the two fathers of her children. She also is on public assistance. All seven family members have had health issues that require frequent visits to the local clinic and hospitals. For example, José has had several mental health episodes requiring psychiatric hospitalizations, and ten-year-old Isaiah has severe ear infections that cause bleeding and require draining tubes. José also receives disability, as he cannot work due to mental health issues. Sulia and her children get medical treatment at the hospitals and clinics through Medicaid; Gigi and her siblings get additional treatment (e.g., mental health counseling, eye checkups, and diabetes monitoring) at their school-based clinics. Finally, fourteen-year-old Aracely has an individualized education plan due to a learning disability and goes to a specialized school; as part of that plan, Sulia has to meet the school bus when it picks up and drops off Aracely in front of their apartment building each day.

While the family does appear to get a significant amount of services from these institutions, the process of securing them does not always go so seamlessly, especially when it involves dealing with multiple institutions for the same issue. Consider just a few of the Hernandezes' institutional experiences, of which the first two pertain to sixteen-year-old Gigi. Gigi is about five feet, five inches and slightly chubby, wearing glasses and no makeup, with her hair pulled up usually in a messy bun. She is not one to shrink away from challenges, as she is a confident, opinionated, and academically motivated eleventh grader. She talks often about her plans for college and participates in extracurricular activities such as cheerleading at her public high school (which is an hour away by subway). But when she tries to apply for a summer youth employment program funded by the city, paperwork issues in different agencies foil her efforts. She tells me that the school nurse printed out her record, which said she had a disability. While it was an error in her file, they need to clear it up before her application can proceed. The program also needs proof that she lives in her apartment, but Sulia can't find the copy of the lease that has her name on it. A third institutional obstacle is that her mom was supposed to make an appointment with a doctor to get a work clearance, but they missed one deadline for that paperwork. While any one of those paperwork snafus could be rectified with time and effort, Gigi and Sulia give up due to the financial constraints in not having enough subway fare ($2.75 one way) to go back and forth to the various agencies to get the paperwork; Gigi's school-issued subway card only allows three rides per day, two of which are needed for her to go to and from school. Gigi ends up babysitting for her aunt, who lives in Connecticut, but does not get paid for her efforts or obtain any work experience to put on her résumé for future job prospects or college applications.

Gigi also has been adjusting to managing her newly diagnosed type 2 diabetes and gets treatment for it at a community clinic across the street from her apartment. The clinic is affiliated with St. Simons Hospital, a fifteen-minute walk away from their house, where her uncle, José, goes during his psychiatric episodes. The clinic doctor, Dr. Peters, initially referred her to Weingart, another hospital that has a more specialized diabetes center. This time, though, Dr. Peters referred her to an endocrinologist at St. Simons because her mother, Sulia, said it was too difficult and confusing to deal with the doctors at Weingart. However, no one at St. Simons seems to know she is coming on the day of her appointment. When they get there, the staff send them from floor to floor, as they try to find the pediatric clinic in the hospital. My research assistant, Jerry, who is meeting them there, also has a hard time knowing where to go. When he finally finds them, he recounts the following interaction with the medical staff in his fieldnotes:

> A man shows up at the door, although he did not sport a white coat, I [Jerry] assume he is the doctor, according to the authority he exercises in asking questions. The man doesn't introduce himself, nor does he ask me who I am or what I'm doing here. He confirms Gigi's identity and says: "Sorry we can't see you here" in a thick accent. Sulia and Gigi inquire in confusion and he says that he doesn't have the team here to give her what she needs. He asks: "You have diabetes, right?" Gigi responds "Yeah," slightly annoyed, wide eyed, and with a nod. He says: "We don't treat diabetes here; you need to go to Weingart." . . . The man proceeds to ask a series of questions, which seemed to serve two purposes: one, to assess if there needs to be some immediate medical intervention for Gigi's diabetes, and two, to give them the sense that they did not travel all the way to the clinic for nothing. He then says something indistinctly and repeats it frustratingly, moments after Gigi didn't seem to understand. He says: "Are you taking Metformin?" Gigi and Sulia respond "Yes" in unison. "How much? 500 or 1,000?" Sulia says: "100." The man then responds by saying: "No there's only 500 or 1,000, it's probably 1,000 then. Are you measuring your blood sugar?" Gigi lets out a firm yes in much of her responses, she also nods when he asks her if her blood sugar has been normal. He then concludes with: "You need to go to Weingart, there is a dietician and everything needed to treat you over there. Call your doctor and ask him for an appointment at Weingart." I then interject by saying that Dr. Peters told them to come here. As Sulia and Gigi agree, the man shrugs.

Gigi's treatment gets caught up in the confusion of institutions with multiple departments that do not necessarily work together (e.g., the community clinic and the pediatric clinic within St. Simons hospital) and institutions' partnerships with outside agencies. That is, the "partnership" between the two hospitals, St. Simons and Weingart, actually has compromised the care for Gigi's diabetes, as the person in the former hospital assumed that she should have gone to the latter one to see the specialist, despite Gigi and Sulia's protests otherwise. As Jerry noted, the man never identified himself but insisted on verifying Gigi's condition, as if to assert his power over the interaction and to claim legitimacy in his subsequent questioning of their presence. He also seemed to undermine their credibility by correcting Sulia's answer about the amount of medication that Gigi was taking (Metformin). But it was not Sulia and Gigi's "misunderstanding" that led to this situation. Even if they said the incorrect dosage, that did not mean they didn't know where to show up for this appointment. Jerry, who is a Latino medical student, also told the person that Dr. Peters did send them there, but the staff person dismissed his words as well.[2] Whatever the cause of the confusion, the fact remains that after months of not being tested, Gigi's diabetes was still untreated, the family was left frustrated with yet another appointment to make, and they were implicitly blamed for showing up in what was deemed to be the wrong place.

The Hernandez family has had several past institutional experiences that affect how they deal with their current involvements and by extension, illustrate how institutions drive family poverty. Sulia recalled her experience trying to get child support from the father of her oldest daughter, Katy, in discussing her view of how to approach the father of her younger three children. When I asked her in an interview if she went to family court to get child support from the father of the three younger kids, she explained the challenges and her perspective:

Sulia: Yeah, we did, I don't know, I guess he's [Gigi, Aracely, and Isaiah's father] working with a different social [security number], I don't know what. They can't find him. . . . Once they find out his real social, whatever, he, he's gonna be busted good and then he have to pay all that (laughing) no matter what. . . . They'll probably catch up to him and then he has to pay everything, 'cause that was the same thing I was going [through] with my oldest daughter until they found him [Katy's father]. . . . He did something stupid; he went to, he had a car accident, then he filed for disability. That's when they caught him. . . . They wrote me a letter, a letter saying that they caught him and but since she's [Katy] already in time to turn eighteen, they just gonna give her like a credit card, something in her name and that money, they gonna put it in that card, so she can take it out herself. . . . And he has to pay, he has to be putting in the money so she could take it out until she's 21. . . .

Leslie: When did you try with her [Katy's] dad, like how old was she when you tried?

Sulia: That was a long time ago, I think that's when I applied for public assistance . . . [which] gets the order from family court to get his information just to make sure before they start giving me, before public assistance gives me the money, to see if they will track him down.

Sulia believes the system will "catch up to" the father of her three younger children, as it did with the father of her oldest, even if he is able to evade the court by not using the correct social security number for his job. Her reasoning is based on her experience with the father of her oldest daughter, who was caught when he filed a disability claim on a separate incident. While Sulia did eventually see the agency order Katy's father to pay, she was never sure if or when that money would come to her and Katy, making her financial situation even more precarious. Moreover, she is describing different institutions here as if they are all one system. She refers to these agencies as a collective "they," which could include family court, public assistance, and disability, even though each system has distinct jurisdictional boundaries and tasks. Her sense of the institutions as "they"—whether coordinated or not—leads her to connect the previous experience to her current one.

These three experiences are just some of the institutional encounters that poor families like the Hernandezes must navigate as they try to stay healthy, have enough food on their table, and keep a roof over their heads. But they should not be seen as unique to the Hernandez family. Rather, this book shows how the compilation of current and past institutional experiences for a family, versus discrete ones in individual institutions for specific family members, needs to be considered to better understand how family poverty is both mitigated and exacerbated by the many institutions working with them. This book specifically looks at how the institutions play a role in creating those outcomes for poor families, as they set up systems that are inflexible, opaque, or not cognizant of the nuanced and multifaceted ways that families respond to different institutions and situations over time.

CHAPTER I

Introduction

This book seeks to capture a more complete picture of families' lived experience in poverty and, more specifically, how their multi-institutional involvements can perpetuate poverty. While we know a lot about how poor families interact with individual institutions, we do not have an adequate grasp of how their experiences dealing with multiple institutions create a maze of obligations that shape, instigate, and turn on one another. Families spend a lot of time trying to navigate these institutions, which could be means-tested welfare programs (e.g., public assistance, Medicaid), available to all (e.g., public schools), or selective (e.g., criminal justice system, child welfare). Even if the institutions are not able to address or resolve the families' issues, the families continue to seek help from them, just as those institutions initiate and expand their interventions into those families' lives. Based on fieldwork conducted in New York City from 2011 to 2017, I explore these issues by studying sixty-three primarily poor minority families' experiences in public institutions. The book unpacks their experiences to understand how institutional entanglements happen, as well as the repercussions of such interactions for the families.

To illustrate what I mean, let's go back to the Hernandez family discussed in the prologue. Sixteen-year-old Gigi's failed attempt to apply for a city-funded summer job program points to how a "checklist" in many applications might prove challenging for many poor families, given the increased burdens of paperwork (e.g., leases where their names may or may not be on them, as they move often to live temporarily in different households) and financial costs in gathering and taking the forms to all the necessary offices. Gigi's delayed treatment for diabetes is not only due to a lack of effort by her or her mother, Sulia; the hospitals' lack of coordination and discounting of the family's words led to the clinic not honoring Gigi's appointment that day. And while Sulia appears to be passively waiting for Family Court to get child support from her younger children's father, further adding financial strain to her household, she is simply following the course of her previous experience with the same court in the case of her older daughter's father. These institutional experiences are just a few of the many that cumulatively shape Gigi and Sulia's ability to move out of poverty, as Gigi's college prospects and long-term health are affected and Sulia supports her children by going on public assistance and living in overcrowded conditions in her parents' apartment.

MULTI-INSTITUTIONAL MAZE

I use the idea of a "multi-institutional maze" to depict poor families' experiences in social control institutions, specifically in how families get propelled into continued and additional institutional involvements. By "social control," I refer to institutions that have some level of expectation regarding eligibility and compliance in the distribution of services. In this sense, I am not distinguishing institutions by whether their orientation is helpful or punitive or by the family's participation being voluntary or coerced. Indeed, many of the families themselves do not distinguish these institutions by such criteria; rather, they see them as the same type of institution—that is, one in which they do not necessarily have control over the process or outcome.[1]

The maze has several paths, with more than one entry and exit point. Those paths are not necessarily preset but rather evolve out of institutional obligations that open or close points of entry and exit. The families' experience is based on how they know or decide where to turn at which points in the maze. Yet the walls of the maze often prevent families from knowing what is on the other side. Institutional staff play a key part in the families' choices, as they instruct families about what to do. Even if we assume the staff's advice is sufficient to address the family's case in their respective institution, it may interfere with or complicate the families' cases in the other institutions, thereby raising the walls or creating new paths in the maze as the family proceeds.

The complexity of the multi-institutional maze becomes more evident when considering the following tasks and expectations for the families to meet in each institution:

1. *Appear when asked*: Agencies set the appointment times for families mainly based on the staff's availability and convenience. For example, the juvenile court informs families when the next hearing dates will occur and expects them to show up. Schools have set days for parent-teacher conferences, open houses, and enrollment sessions. There is some variation in this regard, such as families being able to schedule medical appointments. Yet even then, some appointments are dependent upon medical specialists' availability.

2. *Fill out paperwork in certain way*: Each institution has its own set of forms that has a "correct" way to be completed; again, there is variation in how intuitive or user-friendly those forms might be, depending on the task (e.g., Supplemental Security Income verification or food stamps) and format (English-only or translations; internet-based or paper only). But ultimately, the outcome of the case often rests on the information listed on the form.

3. *Bring certain kinds of documentation*: Requesting services or demonstrating compliance often requires more than just the family's word or what they put on an agency's forms. The family often needs to provide documentation *before* that issue can be addressed (e.g., medical examination for school enrollment; proof of residence for public assistance), which may not always be readily available.

4. *Prepare for appointments*: In addition to documentation, families might have tasks to complete in advance of their interactions with institutions such as fasting before a medical test. These activities also could involve formal or informal avenues of information seeking, such as parents asking their youth's lawyer or probation officer what to expect in a court hearing or asking their friends or acquaintances (in some cases, searching the internet) about treating a medical condition.

5. *Share information with staff*: Families need to work with staff from various institutions to fulfill the requirements of one institution, such as providing medical notes for school absences or missed court appointments. That process requires knowing what to share when and with whom, as well as being willing to share

that information. It also means being able to get that information from the institutions.

These tasks are not just mundane obligations to be completed for a discrete moment or goal. Not showing up or filling out forms incorrectly could lead to a denial (or at the minimum, a delay) in important benefits that the family needs, such as public assistance, housing, or health care. In short, navigating the multi-institutional maze is different from negotiating bureaucratic red tape in a single institution in three distinctive and interrelated aspects. First, there is an interdependence of peoples' institutional involvements. For example, a youth's visit to a hospital for medical care might lead to a child welfare case because the health care workers are mandated to report suspected cases of child neglect or abuse; alternatively, not informing a probation officer about a youth's school trouble could lead to a more negative court response to the youth's delinquency case. Second, given that interdependence, people's decisions about cases in individual institutions may be more consequential than they might initially realize, such as submitting incomplete paperwork to Supplemental Security Income, causing cutting off of payments, which then affects the family's ability to pay rent. Finally, families' experiences in the maze become complicated due to what I call "institutional mismatch," where the services cannot address adequately the families' issues and yet the institutions still insist on working with families.[2]

CENTRAL ARGUMENT

The book argues that to better understand family poverty, we need to pay more attention to how poor families get trapped in the multi-institutional maze. That outcome is not automatic or straightforward but rather a result of an interplay between families and institutions. The book's focus is not only on the families' actions and views, but also on the role of the institutions in creating unforeseen challenges for the families. That is, the combination or sequence of institutional involvements is not always known in advance. In addition, some problems get resolved and others don't; that unclear outcome could be the result of families' choices, their interactions with institutional officials, or institutional mismatch (or some combination of the three). Thirdly, families vary in how they seek out or resist institutions, sometimes having both reactions to the same institution at different moments. Finally, institutions are not always working in coordination with one another. As a result, the families' experiences in the maze can be unpredictable.

To clarify what I mean by *trapped*, it is the sense of being stuck between several systems with no clear sense of how to resolve any of the issues involved. If the maze is unpredictable, there cannot be a preset roadmap to guide people as to what to do next. At the same time, I am not suggesting that getting trapped in the maze means that there is never a way out. One might exit out of the maze after untangling the ambiguities created by the multiple institutional involvements to resolve the cases, whether that is to close the case (e.g., juvenile delinquency), validate one's eligibility for services (e.g., public assistance, public housing, or special education), or have families give up pursuing any help from these institutions.

The book focuses on the variations in how poor and minority families experience and become trapped in the multi-institutional maze. To do that, I analyze four factors that shape those experiences:

1. *Simultaneous involvements*: Perhaps the most commonly understood challenge in dealing with multi-institutional involvement, this factor affects how families get involved in and are propelled into multiple institutions. New walls of the maze might be constructed with varying heights or knock out other walls, depending on how those institutions work together with one another as well as how the families make their own assessments about which ones to prioritize and in what ways.

2. *Past involvements*: Many of us think of "family history" or "past records" as indicating a higher risk or growing severity of a problem. Yet this book focuses on how families invoke previous experiences—whether with the same institution or same member of the family—in their current institutional interactions. This approach opens up a more nuanced view of how families understand and choose to interact with institutions for different issues.

3. *Multi-household involvements*: This factor refers to families managing involvements for various kin who may or may not live in the same household. It helps to broaden our understanding of the particular challenges that poor families face, given the fluidity of their households due to poverty (e.g., unstable housing, underemployment) and limited resources to handle these types of multi-institutional involvements.

4. *Contingencies in the maze*: Navigating the maze successfully necessitates a somewhat elusive combination of circumstances where families and staff clearly communicate with one another about the institutional requirements and the institutions have

the resources that enable the families to meet those expectations. Most families' situations do not lend themselves to such circumstances, containing contingencies such as mental health issues that make their experiences in the maze even more harrowing and prolonged.

These four aspects provide a richer context to understand how poor families interact with institutions and face more varied outcomes than anticipated. Again, the maze's walls and exits cannot be predetermined, nor can the family's journey through it, given these four factors and the features of the maze as described in the previous section. In sum, this book recognizes that while the ultimate outcome might be that most of these families stay poor, institutions do not always work in tandem with one another, and some actually do resolve a family's issue; again, these co-occurring dynamics lead families to continue seeking out services in some institutions over time. The maze helps us see that complexity as spread across multiple issues and multiple family members and allows us to capture the extent of family efforts dealing with more forms of institutional surveillance.

RACE AND CLASS IN THE MAZE

One could envision how families, no matter what their socioeconomic or racial advantages may be, enter the multi-institutional maze as they navigate various systems (e.g., school, health, mental health) to advocate for a family member with complex problems that may or may not be resolved. Yet families differ in how they choose or are pushed into the maze and also in how they can exit or get stuck in the maze. For example, some middle-class and white families voluntarily might seek out treatment and medication for a youth's attention deficit/hyperactive disorder (ADHD) from a private psychiatrist, while some poor and minority families feel forced to do so by a school that threatens to call child welfare for child neglect if they do not.

Yet while any family might have to go through this type of institutional experience, poor and minority families are more vulnerable, as they have fewer alternatives if the institutions fail to address their needs or if they resist said institutions' "suggestions" for help. In particular, they face three unique challenges. They typically have to deal with more than one institution at the same time for the multiple problems created by poverty and systemic racism, while other families might only have

one issue or institution to resolve that issue. Secondly, the quality of services might differ for poor and minority families engaging with public
agencies compared to the private institutions to which the middle- and
upper-class white families might turn and pay for enhanced and more
specialized services if they are not satisfied with the public ones. A third
and important difference for poor minority families relates to their level
of agency in the process. They generally are not in control of this process, as they receive help from these institutions and often are forced
to deal with them to "fix" some part of their family life (e.g., criminal
involvement among some of its members, child endangerment/neglect,
or a medical condition for youth).

This book argues that poor and minority families are at risk of fall-
ing into this maze and are also harder pressed to be able to get out of
it compared to most middle-class and white families. While all families
might experience extreme levels of stress, frustration, and anguish in
dealing with these institutions, middle-class and white families might
experience an intermittent—albeit infuriating—institutional involvement
for a specific issue (e.g., a delay in a child's early development or a parent's challenging health diagnosis). They also can advocate and persist
more effectively for their own views, based not only on their efforts but
also on how the staff perceives and validates those efforts. As a result,
they do not often experience the enduring kinds of involvements that
many poor and minority families do, which is the focus of this book.

DATA

I conducted fieldwork with sixty-three primarily poor families of color
in New York City from 2011 to 2017. I recruited families from three
agencies working with adolescent youths: two that ran diversion programs for teenagers with delinquency cases in juvenile court and a
hospital that treated teenagers with chronic illnesses such as asthma,
diabetes, or obesity.[3] The families in my study both sought help from
or were compelled to interact with institutions for a variety of issues
such as cash and food assistance, health and mental health conditions,
school troubles, and housing. Given all of those situations, it is not
surprising to find that the families have multiple institutional obligations. Over half of the families (56%) reported three to five institutional
involvements (past and present) and 17 percent reported six or more.
Table 1 shows a more detailed description of family multi-institutional
involvement, based on ten of the sixty-three families with whom I spent

TABLE I INSTITUTIONAL INVOLVEMENT BY FAMILY

Family	Parents (age if known;[a] race ethnicity)	Children (ages if known; italicized in household)	Child Welfare	Church	Disability	Drug Treatment
Bryant	Catherine (51; Black)	*Shawn (15)*, *Edward (13)*, *Rodney (5)*	X	X		X
Cabrera	Sofia & Diego (44, 48; Latinx)	Henry (21), *Mark (19)*, *Richard (16)*				
Fouskas	Eileen (45; white)	Joey (22), Patrick (13), *Brian (10)*		X	X	
Hernandez	Sulia (45; Latinx)	Katy (25), *Gigi (16)*, *Aracely (14)*, *Isaiah (10)*			X	
Garner	Viola (54; Black)	3 sons[b] (28, 26, 20), *Annette (16)*, *Starr (14)*		X	X	
King	Jessica (45; Black)	*Ashley (29)*, *Shannon (13)*, *Bryson (16)*				
Lopez	Leisy (50; Latinx)	5 sons[b] (35, 33, 28, 23, 22), Daisy (25), *Kobe (15)*	X		X	X
Thomas	Talia (36; bi-racial) & Michael (Black)	*MJ (17)*, *Samuel (16)* *Aliyah (14)*, *Mia (5)*	X	X	X	X
Velez	Lita & Juan (60; Latinx)	Rosie (35), *Albert (30)*, *Isabel (15)*, *Peter (11)*	X		X	
Wilson	Michelle (41; Black)	*Shakera (14)*, *Kevin (2)*	X	X		

a. Ages listed in parentheses for both parents and children are based on the person's age at the start of the fieldwork period.

b. For a list of these children's names, see Appendix B.

HIV/AIDS	Hospital/Medical Clinic	Housing	Justice System	Medicaid	Mental Health Agency	Public Assistance	School
X	X		X	X	X	X	X
	X		X	X			X
	X		X	X	X	X	X
	X	X	X	X		X	X
	X	X	X	X		X	X
	X		X				X
	X	X	X	X	X	X	X
	X	X	X	X	X	X	X
	X	X		X	X		X
	X	X	X	X			X

more time over a period of twelve to twenty-two months (all names are pseudonyms).

The average institutional involvement by category was eight for these families. A single type of involvement could refer to several distinct institutions or types of aid. For example, "court" could be family or criminal court, and all the related agencies such as youth detention homes, jails, prison, probation, treatment agencies, and diversion programs. "School" could mean a situation (e.g., learning or behavior issues) requiring parents' attention beyond basic educational support. "Child welfare" could involve several types of neglect (e.g., educational, medical, general) or abuse (e.g., physical or sexual). "Health/medical clinic" refers to multiple health agencies for one person and/or their family members in the household.[4] Finally, public assistance could refer to cash benefits, food stamps, or housing assistance. When considering the number of distinct agencies working with families, the median involvement increases to fourteen.

The parents/legal guardians in my study were primarily Black and Latinx (36% and 50% respectively), with the rest being non-Hispanic white (6%) and other/multiracial (8%). The median age of parents/legal guardians was forty-four years old, with a range of twenty-four to seventy-four. The families reported an average of three children (range one to six) living in their households at least part of the time, for whom they were in charge of their daily needs and institutional involvements; these children could be their own biological or stepchildren, grandchildren or nieces or nephews.[5] The age range of the children was one to twenty-nine years, with boys making up 61 percent of the sample.[6]

Regarding families' socioeconomic status, I classified seven as middle class (11% of the sample) based on families' work status.[7] In those families, at least one of the parents worked in or retired from a full-time professional job (e.g., health administrator, city agency staff, office workers); in one family, the grandmother reported being retired as a health attendant but owned her home and received her husband's benefits. Among the remaining fifty-six families, twenty-five parents (40% of the sample) were not working currently while twenty-nine parents (46% of the sample) worked either part-time or full-time in non-salaried jobs (e.g., home health aides, housekeeping, seamstress, car wash).[8] The middle-class families had on average one less institutional involvement (three) compared to the working-class/poor families (four).

My research assistants and I conducted one-time semi-structured interviews with the sixty-three families, asking them about their experiences either with their youth's court or hospital cases. In total, we did ninety-eight interviews with parents and youths; during those interviews, many of them mentioned other institutional involvements. I also did an ethnography of ten of those families to see how those involvements changed over time and affected their everyday life. The ethnography entailed follow-up interviews and visits with the families over the course of at least twelve months. The follow-up interviews took place every three to four months; I asked families for updates on their youth's court or health case, and families also would mention the other institutional involvements in those interviews. The visits lasted between one to four hours, including home observations; trips to doctors, courts, or other institutions; and family outings such as birthday parties and informal gatherings. I aimed to see the ten families on at least a monthly basis, but the number and timing of visits varied (seven to twenty-one visits per family over a period of twelve to twenty-two months) due to scheduling and communication issues.[9]

In total, 140 visits and an additional 36 interviews (for a total of 134 interviews in the study) were done with the ten families in the ethnography. Finally, I conducted four formal and several more informal interviews with staff in the juvenile justice system and hospitals about the families in the ethnographic part of the study. In the following chapters, I make sure to note if the data is taken directly from interview transcripts; if not indicated, the data is a fieldnote excerpt from a visit with the family. I have described the study design, recruitment process, and sample in more detail in appendix A and have included a list with basic demographic information on the sixty-three families in appendix B.

RELEVANCE TO OUR UNDERSTANDING OF INSTITUTIONS, POVERTY, AND INEQUALITY

This book informs the broader literature on poverty governance, particularly in how we think about the role of institutions in working with the poor. This section briefly discusses three interrelated lines of research in this area: the macro view of institutions as disciplining and punishing the poor, a meso view of individual institutions' work practices through which social inequalities get reproduced, and a micro view on families' experiences in navigating those institutions. This book both draws from and expands upon all of these views, adding another layer to this research on institutions and families, by focusing on the unique challenges of multi-institutional involvement that affect the lived experience of poor families.

The State, Institutions, and Families

This book argues for the need to take a finer-grained look at how institutions could affect family life in somewhat different ways, as compared to the macro view of institutions as a collective force of the state that uniformly disciplines the poor through their interventions that provide "help" and maintain social order.[10] This view generally describes welfare institutions as only giving enough aid to alleviate the most severe impacts of poverty but not enough to enable people to leave it completely.[11] It also sees the institutions as regulating the poor, continually demanding they prove their "deservedness" through rigorous eligibility and work requirements while remaining suspicious about the "legitimacy" of their claims.[12] The lines between welfare and punitive institutions begin to blur, especially in neoliberal governments that assert state authority and control over these clients through notions of individual responsibility to police their "deviant" behavior.[13] In this light, multi-institutional involvement could be seen as a growing form of surveillance or as evidence of increasing punishment of poor families, given mass incarceration and criminalization of welfare.[14]

This book's more detailed look into families' experiences with institutions helps us understand why families engage with them, despite this general outcome of increased surveillance. On the one hand, the book shows how institutions place extreme burdens on families—mothers in particular—whose problems often are not addressed completely. Yet at the same time, those same institutions can be effective and often are the only sources of that help for these families. Linda Blum (2015) frames it as a sort of paradox, noting both the "intrusiveness" of some institutions and the "genuinely helpful" potential of others.[15] Dewey and St. Germain (2016) also see this paradox in their study of women engaged in street sex work; the women acknowledge the positive help from individual social workers on discrete matters (e.g., adoptions of their children) while also viewing the overall punitive character of what they call "the criminal justice–social service alliance" of federal, state, and local law enforcement agencies and nonprofit organizations that generally share the same view of the women's situation as a result of the individual women's choices, versus the social structural factors shaping those women's lives. The pressures on poor families are even greater, considering that they do not have many other options besides public institutions to seek help (Blum 2015). Fernandez-Kelly (2015) further elaborates on this issue, comparing "liminal" institutions that are mandated to provide services but treat their clients (primarily poor families) with suspicion to private institutions with higher-quality services to which middle and upper classes turn for similar issues (e.g., mental illness, health care, education, housing).

This book's perspective complicates the ways that we view institutions' influence on families. The disciplining is not a unified process.[16] Rather, it would be more apt to describe it as a more segmented and incomplete network of institutions that work with families. As such, we need to parse out in more detail how institutions work with families to see which moments lead to increased punishment and which ones lead to adequate support. This book strives to do that nuanced analysis across institutions to show the unique pressures placed on families as a result of the multi-institutional involvement.

Individual Institutions, Street-Level Bureaucrats, and Racial Inequalities

In this book, I also pay attention to the variation in families' experiences across institutions, in line with the qualitative research on how institutional work practices (e.g., paperwork, gatekeeping, resource allocation) reproduce existing social inequalities.

Perhaps the most classic of these studies would be Lipsky's *Street-Level Bureaucracy* (2010/1980), which focuses on the frontline workers in public agencies who are not able to effectively carry out the organization's mandates due to insufficient resources, overwhelming caseloads, and individual staff's discretion. It is through these frontline workers' interactions with clients, as shaped by their local work conditions, that the inequality is reproduced. As Lipsky notes (2010/1980: 6), "the poorer people are, the greater the influence street level bureaucrats tend to have over them." He goes on to explain how those people might react to those bureaucrats' actions:

> It is one thing to be treated neglectfully and routinely by the telephone company, the motor vehicle bureau, or other government agencies whose agents know nothing of the personal circumstances surrounding a claim or request. It is quite another thing to be shuffled, categorized, and treated "bureaucratically" (in the pejorative sense), by someone to whom one is directly talking and from whom one expects at least an open and sympathetic hearing. In short, the reality of the work of the street-level bureaucrats could hardly be farther from the bureaucratic ideal of impersonal detachment in decision making. On the contrary, in street-level bureaucracies the objects of critical decisions— *people*—actually change as a result of the decisions. (2010/1980: 9)

Similarly, Victor Ray's theory of racialized organizations shows how "through daily, routine organizational processes, racial schemas delineating racial sub- and super-ordination are connected to material and social resources" (2019:46).[17] Minority families have limited agency in racialized institutions, which dictate the conditions of their participation and the time they have to spend on their cases; moreover, they face discrimination despite any class advantages they might be able to leverage for services. So, if these institutions disproportionately work with minority families, that further deepens the racial inequalities, as white families have more privilege to either escape or negotiate with those institutions.

With these perspectives, we can begin to see how institutions manifest inequality through the somewhat predictable but not uniform interactions between individual staff and clients, in which the former could decide to exert their authority in powerful ways. The multi-institutional maze shows the repercussions of these individualized practices *across* institutions, as institutional obligations compound one another and the discretionary actions of frontline workers in one agency can affect the work in another, propelling families out of or deeper into the maze.

Families' Experiences

Finally, the book draws from and expands upon the scholarship on families' experiences in social control institutions, particularly in how poor mothers employ their cultural capital.[18] That capital includes the knowledge, resources, and skills, as shaped by their social position, to advocate for their families' needs.[19] Many have focused on one institution (e.g., school, welfare, prison, hospital), discussing how parents' cultural capital can be leveraged for greater or worse case outcomes in those institutions, whether as a result of the parents' efforts or the institutions' assessment of those efforts.[20] Perhaps most well-known in this line of work would be Annette Lareau's study (2003/2011) that found the "concerted cultivation" approach of middle-class families aligned more closely with schools' ideas of motivated students, which in turn, enhanced the youths' educational outcomes and interactions with other institutions. In contrast, the "accomplishment of natural growth" view of poor families promoted more passive students who seemingly respect authority in behavior but not necessarily to their benefit educationally. While these studies provide a rich sense of how inequality is transmitted via institutions, they also employ a somewhat static notion of cultural capital used across all institutions with the same expected results (e.g., poor families' cultural capital leads to more negative case outcomes compared to middle- and upper-class families' cultural capital).

Some studies have painted a devastating picture of families' struggles in navigating multiple institutions. Bowen, Brenton, and Elliott (2019) highlight the institutional conundrums where government aid such as food stamps and WIC (Special Supplemental Nutritional Program for Women, Infants and Children) provide invaluable support to poor mothers to feed their families while also imposing stigmas on them as "bad" or "lazy" parents who are not working hard enough to be financially independent and to raise healthy children.[21] Similarly, Abraham's (2019/1993) heartbreakingly detailed account of one family's attempts over generations to seek medical care for its members' chronic illnesses shows the worsening effect on the family's health (for both the sick and the caregiving members) as it interfaces with several health care providers, Medicaid, Medicare, and nonprofits that appear to be working at cross-purposes within increasing budget constraints and with sometimes intentional neglectful oversight. While both of these studies mention all these institutional interactions on families' everyday lives, they focus on just one issue—food or health—to frame the cumulative effect. Other longitudinal qualitative studies tend to reduce families' experiences to their final outcome of achieving limited social mobility (Seefeldt 2016) or becoming "institutional captives" (Sered and Norton-Hawk 2014) in interacting with various agencies without obtaining any meaningful support to enact lasting improvements in their lives. I argue that we can learn more about the impact of multi-institutional involvement on poor families if we consider how their experiences might vary in strategy and effect across issues and institutions.[22]

PLAN OF THE BOOK

The following chapters unpack the four factors influencing families' journeys in the maze—concurrent involvement, past involvement, multi-household involvement, and contingencies—in greater detail. They each feature a focal family to highlight the main themes, bolstered with examples from the other families in the study that further develop the nuances in those themes. Where appropriate, I will use data from the few white and middle-class[23] families in my sample to highlight the unique ways that poor and minority families become enmeshed in a variety of institutions like courts, schools, and hospitals as they struggle to deal with problems and troubles they confront in their family lives.

Chapter 2 explores the complexity of the multi-institutional maze seen from one point in time. It features the efforts of the Lopezes, a Latinx family, in navigating multiple agencies at the same time for mental health, disability, child welfare, schooling, and housing issues, along with other matters that unexpectedly come up along the way. In particular, the chapter highlights two challenges for families like the Lopezes that arise in this situation. One is logistical, such as paperwork glitches. Another key logistical issue pertains to geographical pressures of being in two places at once, sometimes in multiple states or countries, potentially leading to increased involvements. The second challenge is how involvement in an institution triggers or affects families' cases in other institutions. The chapter also discusses the family's strategies in navigating concurrent involvements, showing that the success of those actions largely depends on how the parents are able to work around, within, or against the institutional rules.

Chapter 3 argues for the importance of understanding families' past institutional involvements to better understand the families' current strategies with institutions. For example, considering previous involvements helps show how any family, regardless of its race or class background, might approach an institutional involvement now with more ease if it obtains some familiarity with those institutional processes. At the same time, intergenerational poverty and race affect family involvement as many poor families of color talked about several generations of family members having the same experiences with institutions with no meaningful resolution, due to the pernicious forms of institutional racism and classism.[24] This chapter features the Thomases, an African American family, where the mother's past experiences in foster care and mental health treatment shapes her approach to dealing with her children's court, school, and mental health issues. One might expect poor families of color like the Thomases with past involvements to have a more guarded or distrustful view of those institutions compared to middle-class or white families. However, that is not the case in many of the families in this study who sought out help from those institutions. Taking this temporal view highlights the need to capture families' unique institutional histories to understand how they approach current multi-institutional involvements.

The fourth chapter expands the analytical lens to consider the ways that poor families often have to negotiate institutional involvements for members living across multiple households. It does so by exploring how the Fouskases, a white family, manage their teenage children's court, welfare, and mental health cases across two households and also assist their extended family members (who live in two additional households) with their own court and welfare cases. Poverty shapes this process, as unstable housing, health issues, and justice involvement subject families to a porousness of household makeup that other families are less likely to experience. The chapter shows how families' attention and resources become more limited in these instances; at the same time, families can use those same situations to exert their agency. I also focus on how these issues become exacerbated for separated or divorced parents living in different households.

In chapter 5, I turn to three contingencies—mental health issues, domestic abuse, and immigration—that affect how families manage and adhere to the many institutional rules in the maze. These contingencies or mitigating factors expose instances of institutional mismatch and the unpredictability of families' journeys. For example, mental health issues expose the cracks and conflicts in different organizations' policies geared to getting families the treatment needed. Domestic abuse—both intimate partner violence and child abuse—is discussed as posing a challenge in two ways: the institutional inability to address those situations effectively and families not disclosing such abuse to the institutions. Finally, the chapter turns to particular issues related to immigration that the institutions may not fully take into account, namely, the conflicts that arise due to the families' experiences of being "lost in translation" in terms of parental expectations of their children and navigation of different institutional systems across borders. In this chapter, I feature two families: the Bryants, an African American family, and the Cabreras, a Latinx family who immigrated to the United States over twenty years ago. The issues of mental health and domestic abuse create and exacerbate the Bryants' multigenerational and multi-household institutional involvements, particularly two of the children's school and court cases, while issues related to immigration shape the Cabreras's approach to their three sons' juvenile court cases.

The last chapter seeks to expand upon both sociological and policy understandings of multi-institutional involvement and its influence on family life, poverty, and inequality. In doing so, we see how the Weberian notion (1968) of formal rationality in these institutions does not appear to be present or effective, as families become trapped in institutional mazes that do not have fixed entry or exit paths. Any policy attempt for more coordinated services, then, seems doomed to failure, as the maze is not based on any consistent logic. That is, despite reform attempts to either streamline services to save money or increase surveillance over the poor to punish them, families still enter and exit out of the maze in ways that no one can predict or control. While some might argue this conclusion is an updated version of the idea that "nothing works" (Martinson 1974), I do not mean to end on such a fatalistic note. Rather, I offer some practical policy recommendations that seek not to recreate previous reform ideas but rather to reduce the walls and to create more exits in the maze.

SUMMARY

This book takes a broader perspective of family multi-institutional involvement to capture its complexity and the implications for poverty. It shows how and why families might change their strategies with the same or different social control institutions and how organizations might interpret those strategies. It analyzes families' *lived* experiences in those institutions to show how these interconnected, yet not necessarily coordinated, encounters occur. Institutional obligations often conflict with one another, making it even more difficult for families to meet them. In these situations, the walls of the maze inexplicably go up higher, making the path forward more confusing. At the same time, this book explores moments of family agency, looking at ways that families "make do" and engage with multiple institutions. Parents simultaneously wanted, sought out, resisted, detested, admired, and got frustrated by the institutional interventions. Studying these experiences over time, from the families' perspectives, helps us identify the moments in which families might become trapped in the maze and also the opportunities where they might avoid that outcome.

This introductory chapter also has outlined features of the multi-institutional maze that differ from what many of us encounter in dealing with one organization or our typical understandings of "red-tape" bureaucracy. It is not just a matter of better coordination between institutions, as some conflicting expectations stem from fundamental differences in organizational missions. There are many possible inputs into any individual case processing (e.g., informal or formal networks of information-sharing, documentation from multiple agencies) that make that process highly unpredictable across many cases. For poor minority families, three challenges arise as they navigate through the multi-institutional maze.

First, they are more likely than their middle-class white peers to enter in the maze, given mass incarceration, poverty, and institutional racism. They also can get caught up in it due to the vagueness and sometimes differing staff advice about the rules across institutions. Second, the process to get and keep services from public institutions is more difficult as poor families constantly have to prove that they are "deserving" and eligible for services in ways that middle-class white families do not. Not only that, but the services provided are also of lower quality than those from private institutions (or even the same public institutions working with middle-class families, who are treated with more credibility by the staff). Third, poor families have less control over the process, in comparison to their middle-class white peers, leading to further disillusionment. All this leaves the poor more at risk of getting trapped in the maze, keeping them from moving out of poverty.

So to understand family poverty and inequality, we need to focus more on the institutions' role in working with poor families versus looking only at the families' actions. To use a game metaphor, the rulebook for the maze is not clear, in some ways not even written for some situations, leading the players (i.e., families) to have to choose between various strategies based on uninformed or semi-informed options provided by coaches and advisors (i.e., staff or friends and family members). Given the emphasis on individual accountability in social control institutions and the fraying social safety net in the United States, it is even more important to have this shift in focus as families appear to be more intertwined with institutions than ever before as they struggle to maintain their eligibility for services and face the possibility that one institutional involvement could trigger other types of institutional oversight. The outcome of this process can be consequential, as these institutions are dealing with people's financial (e.g., food, housing), emotional (mental health), and physical (health) well-being, as well as their futures (e.g., education, job training). The research presented here expands our perspective about the institutional reasons why some families are "worse" than others at negotiating institutional involvements for themselves and their children, which inevitably shape their life chances.

CHAPTER 2

Concurrent Involvement

Challenges in Navigating Multiple
Institutions at Once

When we think of multi-institutional involvement, it is often from the standpoint of concurrent involvements. Counselors use "eco-maps" pioneered by Dr. Ann Hartman (1995) to capture families' involvements in order to identify the supports or strains in their environment, while policy makers discuss ideas for better coordination of services, with one-stop centers and the like.[1] Sociologists have shown the cumulative impact of this type of involvement as effectively creating what Sered and Norton-Hawk (2014) call "institutional captives" who are unable to achieve any kind of meaningful long-term social mobility, as institutions increasingly treat them as undeserving and the clients themselves lose hope for change. Building on those perspectives, this chapter shows how families' concurrent institutional involvements create more paths and often more obstacles to navigate in the multi-institutional maze. It first outlines the logistical matters related to paperwork and geographic pressures in having to be in many places at once. The chapter then turns to another set of complications related to the institutional inflexibilities and incompatibilities that families encounter in their journey through the maze.

This chapter argues against the simplistic notion that we could address the problems created by multi-institutional involvement with a more streamlined approach across institutions, as we cannot predict all the potential iterations of the multi-institutional maze. In addition, given the ever-evolving nature of the maze, there are moments of opportunity for the families to exert some types of agency that could potentially open up pathways out of the maze, at least for some members of the family. As such, the chapter shows how the layout of the maze is not preset with clearly marked exits but rather unfolds over time, cocreated with families and institutions, amid the logistical challenges and often conflicting rules that come with multi-institutional involvements. That uncertain unfolding can propel families further into poverty in that it adds stress to the families and affects their household dynamics, both of which could influence the families' subsequent actions managing their involvements across institutions.

THE LOPEZ FAMILY: GETTING LOST IN THE INCREASINGLY COMPLICATED MAZE

I first meet Leisy Lopez, a fifty-year-old Puerto Rican woman, and her fifteen-year-old son, Kobe, through the hospital where Kobe is getting treated for asthma. Leisy is short and has a slight frame with a little pouch of a stomach that hangs over her often unbuttoned jeans, which are too small. She usually covers up her jeans with a long shirt or hoodie. She doesn't wear much makeup, if any. Kobe is just over five feet, one inch, and skinny, making him look younger than his age. He doesn't talk much, but when he does, his voice is soft.

Leisy talks very fast and jumps from one topic to another and back again, making it sometimes hard for me to follow; I often would find myself getting lost in her train of thought, having to ask her several questions to clarify what she was saying. She is polite and generous, sharing the little that she has with others. One time, she asked if she could buy popsicles from a street vendor for my research assistant, José, and me; another time, she offered a piece of candy to a stranger sitting next to us in the library.

Leisy and Kobe currently live in a two-bedroom, one-bathroom apartment in a supportive housing facility in the Bronx for people with mental health issues. Leisy has depression and anxiety, for which she takes Seroquel and Celexa. Her building is located near a major transportation hub of subways and buses on a busy commercial main street. There are on-site counselors and an intercom system where the staff remind tenants to take their medicine. Their building looks new and has interesting technological features in the lobby (e.g., a screen that shows the latest public transportation arrival times for the trains and buses, as well as the weather) and a nice reception area with new armchairs. There is a security office in the vestibule before entering the lobby. I have to show my ID to sign in every time I visit, even when I am with Leisy and Kobe.

Their apartment is very neat, with an open living room and kitchen. Kobe's room is off the kitchen and is fairly large; it has a desk on one wall, a twin bed and dresser on the opposite side. It has a stuffed Yoda, Legos, and a PlayStation on the windowsill. Leisy's bedroom is even larger, clean and simply furnished, with a queen-sized bed, desk, two dressers (one of which has a small television) and a walk-in closet that does not have many clothes hanging or folded in it. I once pointed out how large the closet is, and she mentioned a friend joked he could put his baby in there as a nursery.

Leisy's six adult children (five sons and one daughter, now between twenty-two and thirty-five years old) live elsewhere; her two sisters live nearby, and her brother and his family just moved to Florida. Her mother passed away the year before; although they had a somewhat difficult relationship while she was young, Leisy says she is very sad now that her mother is gone.

Figure 1 shows her family's institutional involvement, both past and present, based on the interviews and fieldwork I did with this family over twenty-one months. Leisy has had extensive involvement in the child welfare system, both as a child (she was removed from her mother's care for neglect and abuse) and as someone who gave custody of her six other children to her mother when she was battling drug addiction. She also spent time in jail for drug possession. Before getting her apartment in the supportive housing, Leisy was living in a homeless shelter for three years.

Of concern for this chapter, Leisy currently has contact with ten institutions just for herself and Kobe: drug treatment, hospitals, child welfare, mental health agency, disability, housing, public assistance, school, Medicaid, and court. Every week, she is expected to attend a drug treatment program three times, due to an open child welfare case. She told me the hospital initiated that case when she went to the hospital emergency room the previous September for a cut hand; although she explained to the staff that she had been drinking and it was an accident, they thought she was trying to hurt herself. Every month, she has to refill her Suboxone prescription to manage her opioid addiction.[2] This requires a face-to-face session with the doctor at a local health clinic. She also has a bimonthly psychiatrist appointment. Meanwhile she has several medical appointments and tests, most recently to check

Mental Health Clinic Leisy – anxiety	Disability (Supplemental Security Income) Kobe – asthma Leisy – applying	Criminal Court Leisy (probation)
Hospitals Kobe – asthma Leisy – stomach issues	FAMILY (relationship to Leisy) **Leisy** **Kobe (son)** **Fernando (son)** **Tommy (son)** **Javier (son)** **Kenny (son)** **Joel (son)** **Daisy (daughter)** **Carter (boyfriend)**	Juvenile Court *Daisy (truancy)*
Drug Treatment Leisy *(past* and present)		Prison/Jail *Leisy (jail)* *Javier (prison)* *Tommy (prison)* *Carter (jail)*
Housing *Leisy (shelter)* Leisy (supportive housing)	School Kobe – truancy/summer school	Child Welfare (ACS) Kobe (educational neglect and neglect) *Leisy (abuse)* *Fernando (neglect)* *Tommy (neglect)* *Javier (neglect)* *Kenny (neglect)* *Joel (neglect)* *Daisy (neglect)*
Medicaid Leisy	Public Assistance Leisy	

FIGURE 1. Lopez family's current and past institutional involvements (past in italics)

for breast cancer and acid reflux, as well as medical appointments for her son, Kobe, who has asthma and allergies. She often gets confused with the instructions to prepare for all the medical tests (e.g., no eating before some, taking pills for others), which she attributes to the side effects of her mental health medication. She also has to deal with Supplemental Security Income (SSI) for Kobe, due to his asthma, while also pursuing her own SSI case for the past four years based on her mental health issues; she found a lawyer through a street sign, and he has been appealing the initial denial decision for her case. Her reasons for continuing these appeals are partially informed by her involvement in two other agencies: the supportive housing facility, where the other residents have SSI due to their mental health issues, and welfare, which determined she cannot work due to her mental health issues. Finally, she is on probation for Medicaid fraud. During one of my visits to her home, she shows me the paperwork that says she is eligible to file for early dismissal from probation, but she hasn't had time to fill it out due to her ongoing institutional obligations.[3]

LOGISTICAL CHALLENGES TO MULTI-INSTITUTIONAL INVOLVEMENT

Leisy's journey in the maze represents the epitome of getting caught up in "red tape," as she becomes mired down in organizational policies that do not help resolve the intended purpose of her family's cases. Typically, we view the red tape as being confined to one institution and presume that with time, knowledge, and persistence, people often find a way to break through it. However, this section explores two logistical challenges created by multi-institutional involvement—paperwork and geography—that put added pressure on poor families and have implications for their ability to successfully navigate through the maze.

Paperwork

Paperwork seems like a burdensome task that people have to complete and if necessary, redo until it is accepted by the organization. Yet we often do not consider how paperwork in one organization can compromise the case processing in another. Since receiving an initial letter in February from SSI regarding her son's asthma, Leisy is working to maintain his eligibility, which provides a significant portion of her family's income ($500 a month). Kobe has had SSI for years, as his asthma was very serious when he was younger; he almost died as a child and spent several nights in the emergency room. She believes he should still be deemed eligible, since he continues to have flare-ups that she needs to manage. Leisy's understanding of this recertification process is that she needs to do two tasks: (1) get documentation from the doctors at the hospital confirming that he is still being treated for asthma and (2) turn in the paperwork to the SSI office by the end of May. While it seems these tasks should be easy to handle, it is more complicated than it looks, because Leisy deals with people in three different institutions to assemble the necessary documentation: her caseworker in the housing facility, Kobe's doctors at the hospital, and her psychiatrist. She tells me in early March that her caseworker prepared the paperwork, which she needs to get signed by the doctors at the hospital. After that, she can drop off the completed paperwork at the SSI office. In addition, she mentions having her psychiatrist write a letter saying she has a hard time understanding paperwork given the side effects of her mental health medication. She spends significant time asking various institutional actors for help, with her caseworker leading the efforts.

Creating another layer to this part of the maze, Leisy has to deal with paperwork issues in two other institutional involvements at the same time that she is dealing with his SSI case. Leisy was required to switch health care plans through Medicaid in February, which affects where she gets her Suboxone treatment and the types of medications she takes; in April, she needs to get a separate documentation from her own doctor to attest that she needs to keep taking the Suboxone to maintain her health care coverage for it. In early April, Kobe's school informs her that he has had excessive absences (not due to asthma), which leads to a separate child welfare case for educational neglect, in addition to the one that the hospital initiated the previous September. He currently is in ninth grade, having to repeat it from the year before. Here's how she explains what happened as I recorded in my fieldnotes:

> Kobe has not been in school for an entire month, but that is the first she heard about it. She says that the school should have told her earlier and that the computer would have called her to say he wasn't there. She adds later that she should have also gotten a letter or something. She says that he has missed days for appointments, but she has the documentation for that. She then says this affects her ACS [Administration for Children's Services, or child welfare agency] case. . . . She has been going to a drug treatment program three times a week [as part of the ACS case]. . . . She doesn't want this school issue to mess up her case. They were about to close it and now this happened.

The delayed timing of this information is now potentially leading to Kobe being held back again in school.[4] Moreover, it has implications for not just his school case, but her child welfare case, where one of its requirements was for Kobe to be in school. According to Leisy, the child welfare agency cannot close the child neglect case initiated by the hospital until she and Kobe resolve his school issues. Despite these institutional pressures, Leisy still exerts some agency in three ways: (1) she complains to the school officials about their mode of communication with her about Kobe's absences; (2) she has documentation to challenge at least some of those alleged absences as unexcused; and (3) she relies on ACS for help. At a visit a month later, she explained to me that ACS will help Kobe with school and get him new clothes and shoes—she just had to fill out a form.

Leisy's active approach here demonstrates the complexity of poor families' journeys in the maze. They are not just passive recipients of institutional interventions, as can be seen in Leisy's challenging the school's communication policies and leveraging one institutional involvement (child welfare) with another (school). At the same time, it is a mixed bag of interventions, with child welfare both supervising Leisy's parenting after her hospital incident, adding on institutional obligations for her (drug treatment), and supporting her efforts regarding Kobe's school issues. She now has to work with the school officials and the child welfare staff in three different aspects: to find Kobe a tutor to help him make up the work, have him go to summer school, or to decide to hold him back a grade.[5] Meanwhile, Kobe's allergies start acting up and triggering his asthma, leading to more school absences and additional doctors' appointments. The doctor sees him in May and finds his oxygen level is not as high as it should be, referring him to an allergist.

Geographical Pressures of Concurrent Involvement

Managing institutional obligations can prove challenging for any family that has to go back and forth between appointments and in many instances, has to be in two places at once. These geographical limitations complicate the family's ability to maintain compliance with any given institution. This dilemma can become especially challenging for poor families who predominately use public transportation that takes an inordinate amount of time and is not always reliable.[6] Many of the families had to shuttle between providers, sometimes across the different boroughs in New York City, within business hours during the week. Three implications for families' navigation in the maze arise: delayed case processing in one institution, a prolonged journey through the multi-institutional maze, and opportunities for family agency.

Going back to Kobe's SSI case shows the challenges, frustrations, and seemingly impossible task for families trying to meet all these obligations across different neighborhoods. After Kobe's SSI payments stop in June, Leisy appeals the decision. A hearing is scheduled in late September at the SSI office in downtown Manhattan at 11 a.m. to consider her appeal. The letter states that she has to be there thirty minutes before because they start on time. However, on that same day, she has two other appointments in different parts of the city: her monthly appointment with the doctor for her Suboxone refill in the Bronx and a face-to-face certification check for welfare in Manhattan (fairly close to the SSI office). Her dilemma is typical of many poor families who often cannot choose where to go for which services and what times, relying upon public transportation and public institutions. That is, Leisy cannot reschedule the first appointment because she needs to get that medication on that day to treat her drug addiction; if she doesn't get the refill, she will get sick with withdrawal-type symptoms.[7] To get the medication, she first has to have her lungs and vitals checked by a doctor at that clinic, who will then call the prescription into the pharmacy. She also received a letter the day before the SSI hearing to appear at the welfare office for a face-to-face certification meeting. Her plan is to go early to the health clinic to be the first to see the doctor when the clinic opens and then to go to the welfare office after the SSI appointment. She believes it should work out, especially if she shows the clinic staff the SSI hearing appointment letter. However, it doesn't quite work out that way:

> 10:54 a.m.: I call Leisy from the SSI building and she says she is about to get on the train. I ask if she is still in the Bronx [at least forty-five minutes away from the SSI office] and she said yes—the doctor took longer than she expected. I say that the hearing starts in a few minutes and tell her I'm going to ask the reception lady what to do since the paperwork said they can't be late. . . . I then ask the receptionist if SSI will let us in even though we'll be late. She says people are always late, so they should come down. I call Leisy to let her know and she says she's on her way.
>
> Leisy calls me at 12:10 p.m., frantically asking me which way she is supposed to walk. She got off the 4 train at Brooklyn Bridge. I am not exactly sure either so all I can tell her is to walk west, away from the bridge. . . . She calls again to say she is at Warren and Church [Streets]. She's not sure whether to walk down or up. I'm pretty sure it is down but stay on the phone with her until I see Kobe and her. She is super-stressed and smoking. I hug both of them and she takes one last puff of her cigarette outside while saying she doesn't feel well and her asthma is acting up. We walk inside to the reception. I ask what happened at the clinic. . . . She said her doctor wasn't there. She was there before 9 a.m., too.

Already we see that Leisy is at a disadvantage in navigating these appointments. She cannot make an appointment with a specific time at the health clinic. Even with her idea to show up early and show the SSI hearing letter to be seen by the doctor as early as possible, she is dependent upon the doctor showing up when the clinic opens (9 a.m.) for that strategy to work. Adding to her delay in getting to her SSI hearing is the geographic distance between agencies (fourteen miles) which takes at least forty-five minutes to cover by public transportation. Finally, she is unfamiliar with downtown Manhattan, elevating her anxiety as she tries to get to the building as fast as she can. She arrives flustered and, due to her smoking, her asthma is also activated. By the time we get upstairs to the SSI office, we are almost ninety minutes late for her appointment:

> 12:20 p.m.: We go up to the SSI office. . . . There is no one at security (I'm assuming people are all at lunch), but an older white man stops, asks us why we are here and then goes behind a locked door to find someone to help us. . . . He finds an African American lady in her 40s or 50s who comes out to ask why we are there. Leisy explains she wasn't feeling well. I say she was at a doctor's appointment. Leisy asks if they could reschedule. The woman tells us to have a seat; she seems a little confused by it all as well. She is pleasant and helpful to us, not immediately dismissing our request even though we are so late. The waiting room has the security desk facing the back room. To the right of the desk are two video rooms and there is a wall of four chairs opposite those rooms. There is a small table with some magazines by one of the chairs. We sit down on the chairs while the woman goes in the back office to check it out. Leisy says she feels like she is having an anxiety attack. She is wheezing. She rubs her eyes and some stuff comes out; she apologizes for it. I say it's ok. She puts her eye drops in. . . . Kobe is playing a hoops game on her phone.

Even though these two staff members at the SSI office are not necessarily the ones in charge of handling situations such as Leisy's case, they still try to investigate what we can do at this point.

> While we are waiting, Leisy says that she is going to welfare after this on 14th Street [15 minutes away by train]. She got a letter yesterday saying something about face-to-face certification even though she has a scheduled appointment on the 3rd [of October]. . . . I ask if she brought that paperwork since she was going to the office afterwards. She says she didn't have the paper with her. The man called her while she was on train and then when walking over here. She says she didn't have pen or time to write down the number but when she tried to call back, the number was not receiving calls. She asks why they do that—especially when she didn't have enough time or a pen to write down the number. She also got notice for her own SSI hearing. . . . She is going to get all the paperwork ready to send to her lawyer's secretary.

Again, Leisy does not appear to have any control over when she goes to the welfare office, as she was informed the day before to come for a certification. In addition to the last-minute notice of this meeting that gives her no time to reschedule, Leisy is not sure why she has to go, as she has another hearing already scheduled for the following week. To further exacerbate her anxiety, it appears "the man" from welfare called her twice about the appointment on the way to this SSI hearing, but she isn't able to get back in touch with him.[8] Meanwhile she mentions yet another institutional task of assembling paperwork for another hearing for her own SSI benefits. She continues to say how stressed she is while we wait:

> She says, "Please, God, let this work out." She says she is having an anxiety attack. . . . Kobe says he is hungry—Leisy says she needs to take care of this stuff first. I explain [to Kobe] that the appointment was at 11 a.m., which is why she is stressed. He didn't seem to know that and says okay. He goes back to playing the game on her phone.
>
> The security officer comes into the reception area. She says we need to register with her. I tell her someone is back there trying to help. She says we still need to register with her. Leisy and I go up—with Kobe's guest pass as well—to say that we are here for the 11 a.m. hearing. . . . She asks Leisy how old her son is. Leisy responds he is 16. The security person says Leisy can try to reschedule and they usually do. The social security hearing officer is only required to wait an hour.
>
> The African American lady comes back out and the security guard says something like "oh, her" after we said she was helping us. The lady is relieved the security officer is back because she didn't know how to deal with video conferencing.

From the setup of the office and the statement that the lady said to the security officer, it looks like the hearings take place via videoconferencing in the rooms off the waiting area. Throughout this whole process, Kobe remains fairly oblivious to the reason for Leisy's anxious state. There appears to be only one person—the security officer—who knows what to do. It also appears there is some flexibility in rescheduling even though the hearing letter explicitly said otherwise. However, the process to do that is not so smooth:

> Around 12:50: The woman helping us now is talking to the security officer, saying to call Bob, and gives an extension. . . . The security officer says on the phone that we were late but came 15 minutes ago, so how can we reschedule? She repeats that we need to call the number on the back of the letter. Leisy sits down in the chair by the table in the waiting room to call the number on the back of the letter right now. Kobe says there is no internet so she can't call. Leisy says she will just try. He keeps insisting but I ask if her plan requires the internet to call. He says he thinks so. Leisy says she can go outside to call but I offer to call with my phone just now. Leisy asks me to talk for her. I am putting in the extension while she tries to talk to me. I dial the extension again and get someone [on the phone]; he seems very calm and tries to find the caseworker. He comes back after a few minutes to say she probably is still at lunch so call back in 20–30 minutes. He gives me her direct extension and name (Ms. Miller).

I offer to use my phone instead of delaying the call even further by having to go outside to try to find a free Wi-Fi connection to be able to use Leisy's phone. I speak to Bob on Leisy's behalf after she asks me to do so. He tells me that Leisy needs to call back to another number to speak to the caseworker, Ms. Miller. We leave the office around 1 p.m.

> Leisy decides to go back up to the Bronx, not going to welfare today. She'll wait until later to go there. She'll first go see Ms. Vergara, her case manager in her building, to help with paperwork. She will call Ms. Miller as soon as she gets out of the train. She is now going to the pharmacy to pick up her medicine [Suboxone]. She can take the 2 train up there. We walk to the subway station together, and Kobe asks again for some food. She says she can get him food in the Bronx where it is cheaper. She then says something about not having change and needing to get some for the MetroCard. She asks me where she can find the 2 train. I tell her to follow the signs in the station and point to one such sign for her.

Just focusing on this one issue of SSI shows how Leisy's journey in the maze descends into an abyss as she confronts what appears to be a house of mirrors with no exits. Leisy's concurrent involvements not only compile expectations on top of each other; they complicate and hinder her actions across institutions, which can lead her further into the maze. The unanticipated confluence of appointments on the same day across different parts of the city, coupled with Leisy's lack of familiarity with some of those neighborhoods, exacerbates her stress on the day of the SSI hearing. The heightened stress leads Leisy to smoke a cigarette to try to relax. Instead, the smoking triggers her asthma and she starts wheezing. She also thinks she is having an anxiety attack. All of that leads her to become flustered and not fully present to interact with the SSI officials when she finally does arrive at their office. As she cannot handle any more stress, she chooses to not go to her welfare appointment. Meanwhile, her efforts to get to these appointments distract her from feeding Kobe lunch; however, due to the higher costs of food in Manhattan, Leisy asks him to wait at least another hour until they get back home to the Bronx where there are cheaper options (typically fast food).

Institutions can create this spatial challenge, which could propel families further into the multi-institutional maze. Elliott Nelson, a fifty-seven-year-old African American, tried to navigate interstate issues that affected both his public assistance case and his fifteen-year-old son Matthew's court case. When I asked how his son ended up in juvenile court, Elliott said in his interview:

It was an incident that happened while he was coming from school. I was informed that he was on a bus and he struck a boy, and they took him to the precinct. And they charged him. And at that time, I was down South getting paperwork transferred from New York. . . . We was trying to get public assistance, but I had an open case from down there. And so I came up; being that I was down there when the incident occurred, one of my twin sons had to go to [pick him up].

While Matthew's older brother was able to get him at the police precinct, the question remains as to what would have happened if the brother were not there, or if the police would have only released the son to a parent. Moreover, it is unclear if Elliott could have tried to close the public assistance case in one state without having to appear in person. What is clear is that this multistate involvement did make this family's adjustment to New York harder, as they eventually ended up in emergency housing while they were waiting to resolve the public assistance case. That process took four months to be resolved.

Beyond having to manage multiple appointments in different places at the same time, Ethel Evans, a fifty-two-year-old African American, shares how one institution (e.g., child welfare) dictates the geographical terms of their involvement often without regard to the impact on her family and its other institutional obligations. Ethel is the legal guardian of her sister's four children and manages their child welfare, school, court, health, and mental health cases. In this extended interview excerpt, she talks about how she offered to take her sister's four children after the youngest one burned their house down and no other family member wanted to take them in:

I said okay [to my sister], but understand I'll help you with the kids until you get yourself together. I'll help you. We started court proceedings to do just that. ACS [Administration for Children's Services, or child welfare] came in and they, I had them at the house, they said that I had to get beds for the kids. . . . My daughter and I got rid of the living room furniture and we put air beds in the living room. . . . ACS came in and they were great until some, a certain degree but then they said the house was—how do you say—not um, not safe, um, safe because there was only one exit. And so, they told me I had to go into a shelter. So, they took me from my beautiful two-bedroom townhouse 'cause they said the kids was in the living room and they sent me some place called PATH. We sat in that PATH place for seven days. It was horrible. It was the most atrocious place that anyone should ever have to go to. They took us, going through the process of going to a shelter and each night that they don't place you, they put you into a hotel. The hotels were better than the place they finally sent me to. The first three places they sent me to, I turned down. It was horrible. It was just horrible. Finally, they put us in this place in Brooklyn. I was robbed seven times. The rats came into the window. I don't mean mice. Rats came into the window. You walk into the house; the roaches would fall on you. You open up the refrigerator, you know that plastic, the roaches was lined in that. You opened up the cabinets—the roaches was in there. It was disgusting. No one should ever have to live like that. The room that they had us in was one room. . . . You take me from my home, which had no rats, no roaches. A decent place for them to sleep, and no one's robbing me, to put me in a place like that. We endured in that place six months. . . . They said we had to stay there a year. I said no way, not me. I'm not staying here. With that, the kids were still going to school in Staten Island. Every morning we got up 5:30 to make sure I had these kids to Staten Island to school every day by 8 a.m.

From what Ethel understands, the ACS rules prevented her from keeping the children in her current house due to the "one exit" and the children's sleeping arrangements. In the meantime, she and the children were subjected to unsafe living conditions in the ACS housing placements that were infested with vermin and vulnerable to break-ins. In addition, those placements were not in the same borough as the children's school. That meant Ethel and the children had to commute longer distances to school, getting up at 5:30 a.m. to travel across boroughs and to not be late. So the agency that is working to help this family get back on its feet after the fire instead ends up adding more stress and logistical challenges that affect its ability to function and deal with its other institutional obligations, such as the children's schooling.

At the same time, geographical issues with family multi-institutional involvement could present a small opportunity for family agency. Later in the interview, Ethel describes how she decides which child to prioritize when she is needed in two places at the same time. Her sixteen-year-old nephew, Micah, who already has a case in juvenile court for truancy and marijuana possession, is at the police station, and her fourteen-year-old niece, Shontae, has a mental health appointment.

Micah got arrested again [for allegedly assaulting another boy in school]. . . . When they [the police] called me, I was on my way to an appointment with Shontae—she had a psych[ologist] appointment [that] I would not miss for anything. And so, when they called, I said, "I have a 12 o'clock appointment that I'm going to. When I'm finished, it's an hour session, when I'm finished, I will be there to get Micah, not before." And so, I did just that. I got down there, I purposely sat outside. They asked for my ID. I said, "you know what, I'm going to let him sit here for a while. I'll give you my ID, not right now." I didn't give it to them. I let him sit there. This is not just once, this is twice . . . within a week. Is it sinking in?

It is understandable that parents may not be able to go immediately to the precinct to pick up their child due to other commitments such as work or, as in this instance, another appointment. However, what is important to note here is how Ethel views the situation. She uses her niece's appointment and also her delay in sitting at the precinct as a way to teach Micah, her nephew, a lesson by having him wait longer. Whether or not Micah did learn his lesson, Ethel's action does suggest that families use these kinds of situations as potential moments of agency to reclaim their own sense of control or, in this case, to reassert their authority over their children and the institutional involvement. It is important to consider then how families' perceptions of the institutional rules affect their compliance in those cases.

INSTITUTIONAL INFLEXIBILITY OR INCOMPATIBILITY

The logistical issues of paperwork and geographical pressures—while frustrating and difficult for the families—still in theory could be addressed and overcome if there was better communication and coordination among the different agencies. In contrast, this section looks at the inflexibility or incompatibility of policies across institutions. How parents deal with these issues varies and affects their navigation through the maze.

One Institutional Involvement Leading to Another

One institutional involvement often leads to or affects other institutional involvements. Figure 2 shows what the maze would look like if we were to try to visualize the timeline of Leisy's experience of trying to maintain Kobe's SSI benefits while dealing with two non-household involvements.

This figure shows all the staff and agencies in bold that are involved in some way with Kobe's SSI case. Kobe's SSI case initially gets denied due to the timing and content of her paperwork and the funds are cut off on June 1. That triggers another institutional case—public assistance—to help make up for some of the lost funds. In early June, she shows me the paperwork regarding Kobe's SSI case that helps explain what happened:

> She brings out three manila folders in a plastic bag—papers for all different institutions. . . . In one folder, there were papers from her doctors' appointments and lab results. Another folder with Kobe's SSI stuff, and the third had Kobe's medical card history and other miscellaneous papers.

Looking over the papers from SSI, I see the initial letter was from February saying they would close it in March and then give two more months of payments—with the last payment being May 31. That letter says she needed to appeal within 10 days. . . . She got confused with that letter and the May 31 date, thinking she just needed to get the doctors' paperwork in by that date. She said she didn't understand the timing and was waiting on the doctors to fill out the paperwork. She couldn't force them to do it on her own timing. . . . Dr. Diaz filled out more paperwork saying that Kobe has "moderate" asthma. I can't read it all thoroughly (Dr. Diaz's handwriting is hard to read), but it seems to suggest he is okay. Meanwhile her caseworker, Ms. Vergara [from her housing facility], helped her fill out a paper from SSI about how serious his asthma is; it says that there were no recent hospitalizations, but he did go to a doctor for treatment. There also is a letter from the health clinic where she gets her Suboxone—saying she has a history of mental illness (depression, bipolar disorder, extreme anxiety) and that she has trouble understanding papers.

Leisy does try to keep track of all her institutional involvements in an organized fashion with the different folders. Yet she is unable to meet the demands from SSI regarding the timing of the paperwork. Echoing Victor Ray's point (2019) about people's limited agency in racialized institutions, Leisy does not have the influence to ask doctors to fill out paperwork in her own timeframe. There are two important aspects to point out here. One, she is not filling out the paperwork alone; her caseworker helped her prepare it, adding to her confidence that it should all be fine. Two, the severity of Kobe's asthma could be seen not as an objective medical fact but rather as a matter of interpretation, considering the various institutional actors' views. The doctor says he has "moderate" asthma while also saying he is "okay." The caseworker at her housing facility—while not a medical professional—indicates that Kobe has to continue medical monitoring of his asthma, which could be seen as a way to maintain his SSI eligibility. The SSI agency determines that Kobe's asthma is not serious and closes his case. Moreover, it is understandable how confused Leisy is with all the paperwork and deadlines, especially given her mental health issues that make "understanding papers" difficult, as verified by the health clinic. Regardless of these multiple organizational interpretations, the reality for Leisy is that she faces a tenuous financial situation where she has $500 less every month to cover costs. While her rent is covered by welfare and she receives a few hundred dollars in food stamps, she gets $91 in cash from welfare to cover the rest. One such cost would be her cell phone ($30 a month), which is vital to her staying in touch with all of these agencies, leaving

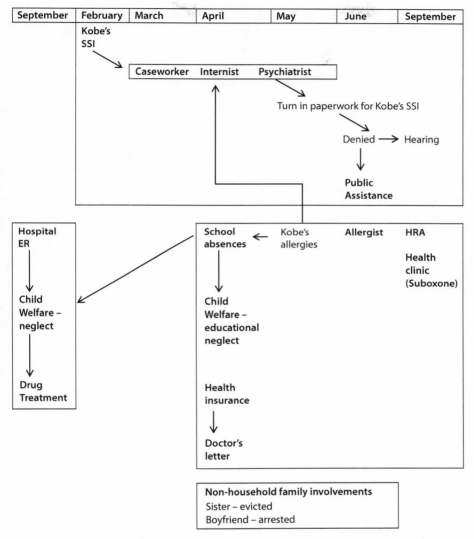

FIGURE 2. Multi-institutional maze for Kobe Lopez's SSI

her with $61 a month for any additional food costs not covered by food stamps and other incidentals.

Leisy's journey through the multi-institutional maze just for Kobe's SSI shows how the logic of one institution does not appear to match that of another. That is, her housing facility accepts people with mental illness like Leisy, but SSI does not view her mental illness as meeting the criteria for disability benefits. Similarly, Kobe's allergy-induced asthma is serious enough for the doctor to be concerned with his oxygen levels yet not enough to continue his SSI payments for asthma. She is doing all that is expected of her, yet what accommodations are we making for someone like her who has mental health issues? Instead of validating all that she is doing, institutions are piling on more obligations and responsibilities, making it harder for her to move ahead.

On a similar note, many of the minority and poor mothers discussed situations in which institutions (justice, hospital, and schools) threaten to call child welfare to coax a parent to do what they want even if it is not necessarily what the parent desires for the child. Two middle-class Latina mothers' experiences highlight how this threat in some ways exists for minority families, irrespective of class. Veronica Diaz, a thirty-five-year-old Latina MSW student whose fourteen-year-old son, Mateo, is in juvenile court for attempted robbery, talks in an interview about how her son's school raised the potential child welfare involvement to "motivate" her to comply with their wishes:

> I think society is so quick for medication and why not test different areas first and feeding them different stuff before we medicate them? You know at one point . . . the school made me feel like if I didn't get him tested [for ADHD] that they were gonna call ACS (child welfare) on me and if I didn't give him medication, they would call ACS on me. I gave him medication for three years for what? . . . They just seem to look at one thing. . . . It took so much to get him out of you know special ed[ucation]. We know he could function on a regular level; we knew he could do whatever, but they are quick to say that he belongs in special ed because of what he did [his charge was for attempted robbery of a kid he met at school]. Really, he didn't do it in the classroom, so you know like they mix all those things together, oh he's a minority, he's from a single-parent home or whatever the case may be. I will not, I will not hold his head over what he did. . . . We teach our kids from early on, he's known what . . . he could have.

For Veronica, the school doesn't consider other reasons except ADHD that explain why her son, Mateo, might be acting out. Veronica used to be a correctional officer, so she is not necessarily resistant to the court intervention; rather, she is dissatisfied with how the school is penalizing him for a non-school offense. She discusses how the school uses other involvements such as her son's recent court case to legitimate its placement of him into special education, which she believes is unrelated. She sees the school's response as racialized, saying it uses her son's racial background and family structure to group together his behavior within and outside of school as all problematic. As a result, Veronica doesn't internalize the school officials' view, insisting instead that they need to look more closely at themselves and also to respect parents like her who are teaching values to their children such as not stealing.

Similarly, Luz Lee, a middle class fifty-two-year-old Puerto Rican mother, describes the dilemma she faces with the school for her eighteen-year-old son, Nolan, who has diabetes. The school nurse insists that Nolan go home if his blood sugars are not in control. Luz views this nurse as incompetent; she makes him drink too much water when his blood sugar is high, which does not help the situation. Nonetheless, Luz and Nolan are subject to the school's rules. She explains in her interview that "the hard thing was—they cannot tell you no diabetic in school, but they try not, they want you there every day." When I ask what would happen if she didn't show up at school, she says, "I would have to make it. If I didn't show up, they probably would call a social worker and have my kids taken away." Whether or not the school would call a social worker, Luz has interpreted these demands as real. As a result, Luz is unable to work because she feels she constantly has to be available to go to the school; she used to work full-time as a finance administrator for a television network. While she does qualify that Nolan's diabetes is an extremely complicated case, she still insists that school could be more efficient in managing his diabetes with this simple guide: "If his sugar is low, he should eat something. If the sugar goes up, he stays in school. If the sugar is high, he should drink water. If the sugar goes down, he should stay in school." However, this constant back and forth between the nurse, Nolan, and Luz has made him not want to go to the nurse because she keeps sending him home instead of helping him monitor his blood sugars and administer insulin on his own. So the school's insistence of involving Luz in Nolan's diabetes management further delays his ability to transition to manage his condition independently. It also leads to more potential school troubles as the principal ends up calling Luz in to discuss Nolan's excessive absences, which are mainly due to the nurse insisting that he go home.

While class advantages do not prevent minority families like Luz and Nolan from encountering institutional child welfare involvement, their middle-class status helps them to get out of the maze quicker or to ignore the threat because of their resources and increased credibility as "good" parents with the child welfare staff. Luz can afford to stop working due to the financial security of her husband's income as a television journalist. In contrast, if child welfare cases are opened on poor families, they have less resources and credibility with which to close those cases. The next section addresses some of those conundrums that poor families encounter.

Caught Betwixt and Between

Beyond facing situations where one involvement leads to another, families find themselves getting caught between institutions, where they cannot resolve one case without dealing with another. For Leisy, it is not just meeting the expectations of one institution but being at the mercy of another institution's expectations. As mentioned earlier, she says that her child welfare case cannot be closed until Kobe is doing better in school. In the meantime, Leisy has to continue going to drug treatment three times a week and get drug tested. She often cannot make all three meetings due to her appointments at other institutions, which requires further documentation to excuse her "noncompliance." Yet her continued ACS case is not due to her lack of efforts but a result of both her son's and school's actions. Leisy says that the current school never answered her calls. She notes that the school won't respond to her but does respond to the child welfare staff. So she faces the potential risk of seeming like a disengaged parent to ACS if they don't believe that she contacted the school. While Leisy is doing her part in trying to resolve Kobe's child welfare case, the school is not responding to her in a timely manner to help Kobe find a tutor to catch up with his schoolwork before the end of the school year.

In addition, the burden of each institutional involvement can compound upon one another, making it harder to resolve any one. So for poor families with more involvements than middle-class families, it then becomes even harder to exit the maze. For example, Leisy can't get off probation because of her other involvements. During one visit, she shows me the paperwork dated nineteen months ago that says she is eligible to file for early dismissal from probation. She hasn't pursued this option because she hasn't had time to fill it out.

> She mentions that she is on probation for a Medicaid fraud case where a girl was selling medicine that she got using Leisy's Medicaid. She [the girl] was selling it for thousands of dollars. . . . Leisy pled to five years of probation instead of going back to jail. . . . She is now in the fourth year. She goes to a kiosk, which scans her hand (she mimics putting her hand on a scanner). I ask if she got to keep her Medicaid. She says yes because she wasn't the one to sell the drugs. She then shows me another piece of paper. . . . It says she is

eligible to apply for early termination of probation but that the judge would have to approve it before she officially was terminated. It lists a bunch of eligibility requirements. She says she needs to bring "her budget." I don't know what she means by that, but I do see a bullet that says, "working, school or in program." I ask about that, and she seems confused what I'm saying. She repeats the budget idea, so I leave it be for now. I then ask if she has any outstanding court fines/fees, which is another bullet point. She says no. I think to myself that the paper is not very clear on what she needs to provide as documentation. . . . She says she plans to go through all her papers tomorrow. She likes to deal with it when things are quiet and calm. She does this every two months to make sure to separate the important from unimportant.

Leisy could have gotten off probation over a year and a half ago but first needs to submit more paperwork to do so. However, as it is too complicated to do it, she leaves it for another time. It is unclear whether or not she will put it in the "unimportant" category of paperwork, given all of her other medical and mental health, school, drug treatment, and child welfare related paperwork. But since she has been eligible to fill this out for over a year and up until this point has not done so, one could assume it would fall into the "unimportant" category. Yet while it is not an immediate priority, staying on probation adds another task for her to do—scanning her hand at the kiosk—among all of her other institutional obligations.

Institutional inflexibilities not only prolong a family's ongoing cases; they add to a family's financial precarity. One mother, Eva Pena, discusses the painful and frustrating experience of trying to work with the court system to get child support, only to be mired in the inflexibilities of its process. She is forty-two years old and emigrated from Argentina as a young child. She lives in an apartment in a two-floor house in Queens with her three sons, fifteen-year-old Pablo, thirteen-year-old Felipe, and eight-year-old Matias. Their neighborhood appears to be middle class, but her apartment is cramped and small. She points out the water damage to her room that has been there for over a year and that the landlord has not yet fixed. Her oldest son, Pablo, was recently arrested for assault after hitting her. She explains in her interview what happened when she went to the court to get child support from her sons' father:

His father . . . doesn't give me child support for four years now—five years. Maybe a year and a half ago, I decided to go on welfare because my work is very slow. It's [her job] beauty, so it's a luxury. You have money, you go. If you don't, you don't. . . . I went to court one day, spent all . . . one day . . . and at the end, I told him, "Oh, I come here to ask for child support." [He asked,] "You on welfare?" [I said,] "Yes." [He replied,] "No, we can't help you . . . if you're on welfare, you have to let them look for it." . . . I said, I did my own research and I find him before you. I have Facebook. I took pictures. He's here. And he's on a different last name, and this and that. I gave you his Social Security number. I gave you his address a year ago. He is on probation so he's in the system. Was arrested and he's on something. So, I know he goes to see probation officer or something. He's on the system, how come you can't find him? It has been now almost a year.

Eva appears to be stuck between the welfare and family court systems. While she works in skin care, she describes it as a "luxury" industry that often can be slow. As a result, she went on welfare to support her three sons. She then decided to get child support from their father so she could stop being on welfare. But according to the person she spoke to at the courthouse, welfare should be the institution that looks for the father to get that child support, not the court. Eva assumes the family and criminal courts are all one "system," in that the father is on probation. However, they are not, and she has been waiting for almost a year for this to be resolved. The irony in this situation is that she knows where Pablo's father lives. However, for the court to take that information, it tells her to either wait for welfare to find the father or get off welfare so that the court could then take the lead and take her information about the father's location. She talks about her frustration with the whole experience:

> I want him to pay my $800 a month, so I could have my things, and not be on welfare. . . . I know where he lives. At least I know where he [is] getting his mail. . . . It doesn't make any sense. So, you tell me—so court [would] rather me to have welfare. . . . okay, I'll go to the judge. You send the letter. Have him come [to court]. . . . No, they [the court] said, "In order for you to do that, you have to leave welfare." So, meantime, how do I—I have three kids I have to feed. They have to eat. They're only giving me $400 for rent, and that's it, and food stamps. That's the only welfare [I] have. . . . I don't wanna be on welfare. I was never on welfare. I don't think I should be on welfare. I think I could work. And welfare, if you work more than thirty hours, they take you out. If you work less than thirty hours, they take you out. . . . I don't understand the system. . . . This is supposed to not be a third-world country, but it works as a third-world country.

Eva appears to be in an impossible situation here. She doesn't want to be on welfare, preferring to work as much as she can. She must decide whether to keep receiving $400 in welfare benefits, versus potentially getting double that amount, $800 in child support, if she first gives up her welfare to let the court take over the search for the dad. However, she can't give up the $400, as she has to provide for her three children now. In addition, to remain eligible for welfare, her work hours are limited to exactly thirty hours a week. For her, this kind of situation feels more like a "third-world" problem, not something that a developed first-world country like the United States would have. So while the path to getting child support seems clear enough, there appears no clear timeframe or flexibility to it, leaving her to "choose" between one of two bad options (e.g., welfare) that takes her down another path in the maze with more rules (e.g., limit to number of work hours) that further limit her ability to exit the maze.

FAMILY STRATEGIES IN THE MAZE

Families often become mired down in their concurrent institutional involvements. Yet it would be inaccurate to characterize this involvement as top-down or one-directional. As mentioned briefly in the previous section, families like Ethel and Leisy's do have opportunities to exert their own agency in these situations, to contest or fight back against the policies. Parents also use institutional involvements to deal with other aspects in their lives, including additional institutional involvements. During a home visit, Leisy described how she approached a school-related trouble for Kobe who was getting bullied by another student years ago:

> Leisy said they tried to resolve it among themselves but the parent of the other kid wouldn't engage. The only way it worked was when she says that they had an "ACS case," threatening to send ACS to the other mom who didn't show up for the meetings. Two boys who were ganging up on him stopped after that point. She says Kobe is a peaceful kid, not looking for trouble or fighting.

While one might question why a parent would invoke ACS (child welfare) on another parent, it does seem plausible that they are simply replicating what institutions do to parents: threaten ACS involvement to influence a family's behavior.[9] Given the fact that the other mother wouldn't engage otherwise, this strategy appears to be an effective option for poor families with relatively few alternatives at their disposal to rectify the situation.

Leisy also uses the rules of one institution to manage her internal household dynamics. Her boyfriend of two years, Carter, creates potential problems for her compliance in her supportive housing facility. He visits her apartment often and behaves erratically. Carter is thirteen years younger than her; she tells me that it feels like he wants a second mom to take care of him. She believes his behavior is due to him being off his mental health medications; at the same time, she does not feel like she can directly tell him what to do. So, Leisy uses the facility's policies to help encourage Carter to keep taking his medication:

> *Leisy:* I gotta be careful because if he snap. And then what? If you don't take your medication, because over here, they already told him. You can't come into the building like that. . . . If you don't, you can't come back in the building. And so now he is behaving. Because he cursed the caseworker. And I didn't know. He just came up from here one morning, went down and went straight to her office and cursed her out. Her and the super[intendent] I was like, Oh my God . . . he can't stay over at night. I told him, this is the last time, bro, because if you fuck [up] now, bro, you ain't coming back in. Sorry excuse my language.

> *Leslie:* No, that makes sense. But that happened before he went to the hospital or after?

> *Leisy:* That happened after he came, oh no, before he went to the hospital. . . . He wasn't taking his medication . . .

> *Leslie:* But he has been back since?

> *Leisy:* He is been back now. He comes to visit. He calls me before he comes. I show the ID because I got his ID there. I show it. I say don't come tough, don't come, nothing.

She uses the institution to bolster her request for him to "don't come tough" to her apartment. Her actions serve a dual purpose: in relying on the staff in this way, she is both managing her family dynamics and staying in compliance with the facility.

On a related note, Veronica, the mother from the previous section who doubted the school's assessment of her son potentially having ADHD, talks about how her son's court case helps her address her health issue. She says in an interview, "I can't wait 'til probation starts; it lets me back up a little bit. I have ulcers, I have ulcers, so it's making them worse." Even though the court case led him to be put back into special education, she sees probation, which comes from his court involvement, as helping her. She believes she will be less stressed and by extension, healthier, now that she has the added support of probation in supervising her son. So, while one might assume that multi-institutional involvement serves as an increasing burden on families; families themselves negotiate among those institutions for their own purposes at times as well if they do not have access to other ways to resolve their situations.

INSTITUTIONAL INVOLVEMENTS
AFFECTING FAMILIES' CHOICES

As one can imagine, multi-institutional involvement not only shapes how parents deal with their current obligations in the maze but also constrains their choices that could potentially help them exit it. Parents often talked about having to stop working as a result of their families' institutional involvements. Lita Velez, a sixty-year-old Latina, discusses her situation related to issues surrounding her two adopted children, eleven-year-old Peter and fifteen-year-old Isabel, who live with Lita and her husband, Juan, and Lita's brother, Martin, in a three-bedroom, one-and-a-half-bathroom apartment in a public housing complex in the Bronx. It is located right off a major subway stop and busy commercial street. Lita talks fast, changing topics and people with whom she is talking, and appears anxious when I see her; she is always shaking her leg as if it is a nervous tic and constantly moving around doing things.[10] She has dyed, short, curly hair and a petite frame. Peter and Isabel are the biological children of her husband's son who had a drug addiction and passed away eight years ago; their biological mother also is unable to take care of them, due to her own drug addiction issues. During a home visit, Lita tells me why she stopped working:

> She worked for a while in Long Island—I say that is far away [from the Bronx] to work. She said she paid her mom to watch her kids and also a van to drive out there. She was going to go back to work when Isabel and Peter were younger but couldn't because she has to take Peter to tutoring three times a week and he also has ADHD which was recently diagnosed.

Elena, Lita's thirty-year-old ex–daughter-in-law, also is not actively pursuing her education because of her housing and her nine-year-old son's specialized school. She explains her dilemma to me during a visit at Lita's house:

> Elena is now in a shelter in Brooklyn. It is a good situation for her. But she can't . . . sleep over here [at Lita's house in the Bronx] because she will lose her spot [in the shelter]. . . . Her son is autistic. He goes to school in Manhattan where there are six students to one teacher and one para[teacher]. . . . She takes him to and from school. Before, his school was across the street from their house, so she would drop him off, take three classes at CUNY–Kingsborough [Community College] before picking him up. Now it would be too hard to do that, given the timing. Also, for her to get financial aid, she couldn't just take one course at a time either. She needs three more classes to get an associate's degree. . . . She mentions her friend (who now works at

CUNY in an administrative position) saying that you can only get financial aid for six years. So even if you take time off, those months count toward that six years.

Elena shuffles regularly between three boroughs—Brooklyn (the shelter, her college), Manhattan (her son's school), and the Bronx (her son's grandmother's house). On public transportation, each one of those trips could easily take an hour or more on a good day. Due to her son's new school in Manhattan, she cannot continue her own education because of the time it would take to go back and forth from Manhattan. She cannot change the location of where she is staying, so she temporarily puts a hold on her education. According to her friend, she faces the danger of running out of time for financial aid if she waits too long. While her friend's claim may not be accurate, Elena believes it to be true, endangering her chances of finishing her associate's degree. She eventually finds an apartment almost four months after that previous conversation:

> Elena moved into her apartment just a couple weeks ago. . . . It's a one-bedroom that is big and bright. She put her bed in the living room—and will still have space for a sofa on the opposite side. She tells me how she found the apartment. The landlord listed it on Craigslist in the no-fee section, saying there was only a $50 application fee. She paid that, but he said he does have a broker who will deal with the application. Welfare paid 17 percent annual rent as a broker fee—almost two months' rent. Elena also paid one month in cash up front—in money orders. . . . [At this point,] she's been in the shelters for two years and had been approved for an apartment for the past 18 months.[11] She just couldn't find an apartment until now. She is looking into getting busing for her son to school. She also needs to find a new psychiatrist for him outside of school.

While her housing issue is resolved, she did have to pay the landlord one month on her own, on top of the funds that welfare paid. That action could be a risky investment if something goes wrong with the apartment. She now has to deal with new issues related to her son: transportation to school and a new psychiatrist closer to her new apartment. More importantly for her chances of escaping the multi-institutional maze, she has to delay her plans to get a college degree, which could lead to better-paying full-time employment.

CONCLUSION

Dealing with cases in multiple institutions can become a vicious cycle of one case leading to or prolonging another in a second or third institu-

tion. Seemingly innocuous situations in one institution can have repercussions that reverberate beyond it. Institutional rules also can present
challenges when families have to navigate between conflicting policies
and geographical distance between agencies. Given this confounding
array of institutional obligations, it is important to recognize the extent
and variation in families' efforts and strategies to navigate this unpredictable maze. Most families find moments to exert agency (appealing
decisions, using one agency's rules against another), making choices
about which institutional involvement to address at what time. So it is
important to not reduce families' actions in the maze as futile. Instead,
we should recognize their tenacious efforts to survive and provide for
themselves.

If families find themselves trapped in the maze, it is often due to institutional policies that create new barriers—whether intentional or not—
that obstruct any path out of the maze. Many of the parents wanted to
pursue additional education or work opportunities but felt constrained
by the institutional rules related to welfare, disability, Medicaid, and
food stamps, all of which were crucial to their family's well-being. And
while Leisy's experience trying to renew Kobe's SSI benefits is perhaps
one of the more extreme examples of a multi-institutional maze, it
does highlight the significant emotional and physical tolls to navigating
it: understanding the paperwork required to apply, a lack of control
over her schedule as she has to wait for the institutions to complete
paperwork and set appointment times, pressures in managing multiple
appointments across different parts of the city on the same day, and
stress. There is also an unpredictability in how the institutions respond
to these situations. There are rules that can't be changed (e.g., the day of
Leisy's health appointment); others that can (e.g., rescheduling SSI hearing); and contingencies that can throw a wrench into the whole process
(e.g., doctor showing up after 9 a.m., public transportation taking longer than expected, friendly SSI staff willing to help despite our being
late, Leisy's anxiety and asthma getting triggered due to the stress). More
importantly, Leisy is not alone in this process. She depends on the staff
to help, even if they are not experts with other institutional processes
(e.g., her housing caseworker filling out the SSI forms). The results of
that labor do not appear successful: while she does manage to complete
one task (e.g., renew her Suboxone prescription), an equally pressing
issue (maintaining Kobe's SSI benefits) remains unresolved. Moreover,
it is unclear what the consequences of missing her welfare appointment
might be. So when families are expected to follow procedures and rules

in one institution, the multi-institutional maze limits their ability to do so, not just by making it harder to navigate but with their actions in dealing with one institution now affecting their status in another.

Ultimately, as this chapter has shown, it is too fatalistic to view that maze as predetermined or endless for two reasons: (1) that perspective falsely sees families as having no power to navigate the system based on their own needs and (2) it gives an impression that institutions cannot do anything to change how they work together. It is more accurate to view the maze as being created out of a combination of institutional inflexibilities and family choices.

CHAPTER 3

Revisiting the Past to Understand the Present

The Temporal View of Family
Multi-Institutional Involvement

Taking a family history usually conjures up the image of a staff person asking about a family's previous experience with the same organization or issue. Yet how to capture and understand a family's past involvement across institutions is not as easy as one might think. Parents may not disclose their previous court or housing cases to the youth's school officials if they don't think that information affects the youth's education, just as medical professionals might overestimate the relevance of an extended member's medical history in how the families respond to the youth's illness. Given that, this chapter argues for the importance of seeing a family's perspectives of its past cases to better capture the implications of them for the family's current cases and its journey through the multi-institutional maze.

This chapter looks at two aspects to past multi-institutional involvement. The first pertains to how families harness information and experience from past cases to shape current ones. Those cases include intragenerational involvements such as youths who have been in court multiple times and intergenerational ones where parents' experiences as children in the child welfare, mental health, and juvenile justice systems influence how they approach similar institutions with their own children. The second aspect considers how institutions view families' past experiences.

The possible influences of past institutional involvements on current cases are not immediately obvious or predictable, yet they do have an impact on the family's navigation through the maze. Given that these influences could be subtle, misunderstood, or unnoticed by institutional actors, we need to consider families' assessments about whether and how they use past experiences in their active cases. In addition, we need to compare those assessments to institutional understandings of families' past experiences; if families do not share the same view of the staff about the severity or relevance of its past involvement for a current case, families could become more institutionally entrenched, as the staff might view them as irresponsible in not taking the correct actions to address the situation at hand. In taking this perspective of families' previous experiences, we see both the cumulative effects of institutional involvement and also the ways that families show resilience in surviving and managing these institutional pressures over time.

THE THOMAS FAMILY

Talia Thomas, a thirty-six-year-old biracial mother, is six feet tall, with a sturdy broad frame. She is well spoken, self-assured, and friendly. When I first met her, she came across as someone who will not be intimidated but also is fair and open-minded. She lives with her husband, Michael, and four children in a three-bedroom, two-bathroom first-floor apartment in a split-level townhome in a quiet residential area of Queens. From the front door, you enter into a large combined living and dining room with a kitchen to the side that has brightly painted walls with artwork and kids' homework hanging on them. The narrow hallway goes back to the bedrooms. Their neighborhood is somewhat remote, with no stores within walking distance and the nearest subway station at least a half hour away by bus. The main forms of transportation are public buses and $2 vans that go up and down the main road a few blocks away.

Talia has four children: seventeen-year-old MJ, sixteen-year-old Samuel, fourteen-year-old Aliyah, and five-year-old Mia. Michael, an African American male, is the biological father of Mia and stepfather for Talia's older three children. Her oldest son, MJ, and two daughters are tall and lanky. Her sixteen-year-old son, Samuel, is also tall but not as lanky (Talia says he is six feet, two inches and weighs 250 pounds); unlike Talia, who has a loud voice, he is soft-spoken when I talk with him. MJ plays basketball and plans to go to college next year. He does have chronic digestive problems; Talia attributes that condition to the fact that MJ's biological father would hit her in the stomach during her pregnancy. Aliyah has autism and is in a specialized school.

I first meet this family through a nonprofit agency working with them on Samuel's court case. Talia has been having ongoing conflicts with Samuel, who she says has undiagnosed and untreated mental health issues. She tried to manage the situation on her own, including efforts to get him treatment on a voluntary basis, which Samuel refused. After the fourth time he hit her during one of their fights, she called the police to file charges, in hopes that the court would then compel her son to go to mental health treatment; he now has a felony-level assault charge in juvenile court. She says the court ignored her plea for help and instead initiated a child welfare case after Samuel's lawyer misconstrued his words about Talia not feeding him enough food. Talia and Michael spent months dealing with that case, leading Talia to give up a job at Walmart to handle all of these appointments and Michael to stop a training program to become a certified air-conditioning repairman. Meanwhile, the child welfare system only focused on the food issue. The court did not focus on Samuel's mental health issues until months later; at that point, Talia and the nonprofit agency disagreed about how to handle his treatment. In addition, Talia points out to me that the court did not help address the impact of Samuel and her fighting on her other three children, or on her as the victim of those assaults. Four years later, Samuel is living in and out of homeless shelters, and Talia, who is separated from Michael at that point, has moved out of New York with her younger children.

It may seem odd to some that Talia sought out help from Family Court only to then not accept its attempts to get treatment for Samuel. However, it is important to consider her past history with institutions. Her mom was not very present for her as a child; Talia then spent time in foster care.[1] Talia takes particular pride in being a mother, especially since the doctors told her that she would never be able to have children after being severely raped and beaten. She also has been diagnosed with several mental health conditions and has dealt with many health issues after getting into a car accident and, most recently, bariatric surgery. She told me once that because she has been through so much and has not died yet, she is trying to not take life too seriously. She says she used to ask God why she was still alive and on this earth but stopped thinking that way because of her kids.

While Talia's family has had decades of interventions by numerous institutions, the question remains how a family's institutional history informs its present involvements. As the rest of this chapter shows, families' interactions with institutions can be informed by knowledge gleaned from past experiences, whether for the same or different person. But that process is not automatic or consistent across families. Rather, with each new experience, the family has to remember, select, and apply the knowledge obtained from the past incident to inform the present.

HARNESSING KNOWLEDGE

Families' Uses of Knowledge from Past Experiences

One way that families discussed their prior experiences pertains to the "lessons learned" on what to do and in some cases, what to do better the next time. These lessons could be practical information about a youth's illness (e.g., recognizing symptoms as triggers for possible medical crises) or about the background information about the institutional process and its specific actors. Regarding the latter, Talia mentions her strategy to go in person to try to rectify a situation with her housing benefits by providing documentation from another agency (public assistance). Talia's approach is based on her past experience with public assistance:

> I call the house phone and Talia answers. . . . She says she didn't remember that I was coming today and that she has to go to HPD [Housing Preservation and Development] and public assistance to clear up some stuff. . . . I ask why she has to go to HPD. She says that they are asking her for papers that she already submitted to them. She says they are assuming her son is a "grown man" because he worked in the Summer Youth Employment Program. I first thought she meant Samuel because I saw him coming back from that after one home visit. She says they are talking about MJ. She says she got a pre-termination letter so now she has to go to PA (public assistance) to get a budget letter. She says that she already submitted this documentation before, but she is going down there to see what they need. She says they did this before when they were questioning her income when Michael lost his job. They (I assume public assistance) said that "no one can survive off this little bit of money" and she got angry at that. She said to them, "I'm doing it" and "don't tell me I'm a liar." She submitted notarized letters from Michael's bosses and also wrote a letter to complain about those workers to the commissioner.

We have to reschedule my home visit due to this unforeseen administrative snafu. She starts by saying the situation is due to a problem with the paperwork that she already submitted. She seemed to think it was complete, but they are overestimating her son's income due to his participation in a citywide youth employment program.[2] To resubmit the paperwork, she first believes she needs to get the same budget letter from public assistance. Yet her approach is not to give up but rather to figure it out and to demand that HPD rectify the situation. Her confidence stems from her previous experience in challenging the people who questioned her income before. That experience informs her approach here, where she needs to devote dedicated time and engage in face-to-face interaction with the agency staff. She first acknowledges that she needs to better understand the situation, which she believes requires that she go to the office to speak to someone in person. She also realizes the time it would take is more than just one day (or one phone call); it will take a few days and at least two visits to two different agencies. Three days later, she gives me an update on what happened:

> She says that it all has been resolved, adding it was "better than I thought" and that the case manager called today to say they will work it out by Monday. Apparently because MJ is about to turn 18 [years old], she needs to bring documents to show he isn't signing up for other things or has an income. . . . I asked where the office was. It's in Jamaica, Queens, which takes a while to get to but is only one bus.

Everything appears to be settled, but she still needs to bring in more documents in person to fully resolve the issue. While she believes she has successfully navigated that portion of the maze, it is not clear what additional walls might appear once she goes to the office.

Given the interconnectedness of institutions, families' knowledge of past experience from one institution can possibly affect how they approach current situations in different institutions. Two years after the HPD and public assistance issue, Talia is planning to move out of her apartment due to continual problems with her landlord, Maria, who now wants to sell the property. Talia and her husband, Michael, separated months before, and she currently has a new boyfriend, Darnell. She decides to move to another state where Darnell grew up and is trying to transfer her Section 8 housing benefits. She says that requires her to physically be present in the new state. However, she now also has to appear in Housing Court in New York City the following day due to what she says is a false claim by Maria about unpaid rent. At first, this appears to be simply a logistical issue of being in two places at once. Yet this fieldnote from one of my home visits with Talia shows it is more complicated, and her past experience with welfare informs her approach to the situation:

> Every year, Maria raises problems saying Talia hasn't paid all of her rent—even though the rent should be paid by both her Section 8 and welfare. This

year Talia is tired of dealing with it and also this is the first time Maria has taken it to court. Talia believes Maria did that because Talia called 311 on her for not fixing hot water. She says you can tell because the court filing happened soon after that call. She has spent all morning trying to figure out exactly what she owes to Maria. She says sometimes welfare doesn't pay all of it, but it is certainly not as much as Maria claims (almost $8,000). She says that a faith-based nonprofit is willing to help pay off the amount, but their max is $7,000. Welfare also said it would pay but wants the correct amount, not just what Maria says. I don't mean to impose but I offer to help her go through the paperwork. She says she was hoping I'd help and goes to get the paperwork. I see Maria's letter to the court, outlining all the payments she claims to be owed. It looks like all of the welfare amounts for almost the last two years. Talia then shows me the paperwork from HPD [Housing Preservation and Development]. It has the agreed upon rent and the amount they will pay. . . . She then shows me two different types of printouts from welfare listing all the amounts of support broken down by category—shelter and general assistance. Finally she shows me her notebook where she has written several columns to outline the different amounts—how much is owed after HPD's payment, how much welfare actually paid, and the difference between the two columns. . . . I go through it all with her. . . . She owes at most $3,995 (but that includes at least six months for which Talia doesn't have the welfare printout sheet, so in fact, the amount could be much lower).

Based on the information Talia shows me, it is understandable to see why she is confused about what she owes exactly. HPD pays the majority of the rent, with welfare paying the difference.[3] However, while Talia does have records from welfare from the past three years, those papers are not up to date. Moreover, she claims they haven't always paid the correct amount in the past, so she is not able to definitely refute Maria's claims about the nonpayment of rent. That past experience with welfare also compromises her efforts to resolve this issue, where she is seeking out assistance from an additional agency (the nonprofit that requires a specific amount of what she owes) and also inquiring both at welfare and Housing Court about the apparent missing payments. It doesn't help that the timing of these institutions' responses and requirements also is not matching up, especially given the geographical distance between the new state and New York City, where she has appointments on two consecutive days. In addition, Talia believes that she needs to provide welfare with the "correct amount" putting the onus on her to keep and maintain all the paperwork, instead of welfare reviewing its records. Either way, the implications for her housing situation are significant, especially now that Maria is trying to evict her.

The family's socioeconomic status can affect how much a family's use of information from its past involvements will influence its current interactions with institutions. Melissa Elliot, a forty-four-year-old middle-class African American mother, has to deal with the juvenile court after her fourteen-year-old daughter, Evelyn, was arrested for attacking Melissa with a butter knife. This is Evelyn's second case, as she was previously arrested for cyber bullying. That case ultimately was dismissed last year. Here is how Melissa describes in an interview what happened the first time in court: "Evelyn was arrested at school for Facebook bullying, which I didn't even know that exist[ed], but it did. That case was closed. . . . We had to go back and forth to court. They threw the court case out, because the people never showed up, which was fine."

Melissa shares how little she understood about the process during Evelyn's first case. She did not know her daughter's behavior on Facebook could be considered an offense. Moreover, she did not appear to be as proactive, noting "they threw the court case out" only after the other people involved did not show up. But for the second case, Melissa talks about how she engages with the court differently. In an interview, Melissa describes her current approach to Evelyn's court case as informed by that past experience, "I saw that if I wasn't an aggressive parent to get her services, where would she be?" She explains more below:

> The key thing with family court is stay on top of them. . . . I told them I want a supervisor and I'm not doing your mediation, your social workers. I'm not doing that, because here's my documentation for the last six months of everything that I have done. So that should be a process that I should skip. . . . I told the prosecutor . . . I need the judge to override the mediation area and go straight and get it. . . . So he put it on her wrapper [file] that [said] . . . instead of Ms. Elliot going to the second floor, Ms. Elliot go[es] to the fourth floor. . . . So I said, "Look, this is what I did." And then the prosecutor brought her to detention.

Contrast that language with the previous excerpt: here, she uses a more active voice in stating her wishes about the direction of the second case (e.g., "I told them I want a supervisor," "I need," "this is what I want") to avoid going through the same steps of going "back and forth to court" in the second case for steps that she deemed unnecessary. She is intimately involved in the second case, telling the court that she wants to skip the first steps of the court process (e.g., informal probation with diversion options such as mediation and assessments by social workers). Her class status works to her advantage here, as she gets the court staff to listen to her pleas to skip the second floor to go straight to the fourth floor and also gets her husband, who runs a counseling program, to facilitate all the necessary documentation, such as an assessment for mental health treatment and medication. Melissa does all of this work because she believes the best place for her daughter is a secure residential group home. Melissa is trying to avoid the situation where Evelyn comes back home but continues to accumulate more probation violations, putting her at risk of a more serious court response. In comparison, the youth from poor families in this study faced similar situations where they chafed under the conditions of probation while awaiting their court hearings and started accumulating probation violations. At the same time, Melissa and her husband still are subjected to institutional interventions; the child welfare agency opens a case when Evelyn accuses her parents of abuse after they argued about her not going to school.[4] While that case was eventually dismissed, Melissa did have to spend a significant amount of time to get it closed successfully.

Comparing Talia and Melissa's interactions with the juvenile court shows the advantages of social class in families' navigation of the maze. Both are mothers of color whose calls to the police triggered their youths' court cases. Both are not immune to the multi-institutional maze, as child welfare cases are opened when their children mention problematic issues to institutional officials. Samuel tells his lawyer that his mom does not give him enough food, while Evelyn tells the school staff that her parents hit her. Both Talia and Melissa deny those allegations. Despite these similarities, Melissa's class advantage eases her family's journey in the maze in three ways. She can leverage her husband's knowledge of mental health treatment to get their daughter evaluated for psychiatric medication and counseling and to also find appropriate group homes for her; Talia remains at the mercy of the court to set up the mental health treatment for Samuel. Melissa also uses her past experience to advocate for, and have the court staff agree to, her bypassing certain preliminary steps in the process of her daughter's court case. Finally, she knows people in the child welfare system to help her close that case quickly; meanwhile Talia's child welfare case remains open the entire time of the study even though an investigator for that agency saw nothing problematic in Talia's home. The key point here is not just that Melissa knows how to maneuver the court system better, as both Talia and Melissa are strong, confident women who speak up about what they want. In contrast to Talia, Melissa has more resources, and more importantly, the court and child welfare staff listen to and respect her words more than they do with Talia.

A family's intergenerational institutional involvement can exacerbate and complicate past involvements' impact on current cases, as it extends the scope of involvement beyond one family member. In particular, parents' own experiences in the same institution can affect how they deal with their youth's case. Yet even here, there is an opportunity for families to harness this kind of previous experience in unexpected ways. Marsha Anderson is a thirty-six-year-old African American single mother of Malcolm, a thirteen-year-old boy, who was arrested for bringing a knife to school; she talks in her interview about her own experience as a child in Family Court for an unspecified delinquency matter:

> [When] I was a child, I went to the courtroom [and said,] "I'm not doing this." I thought I was big and bad and when the court decided my final say and I looked at my mother and my mother was like, "Don't look at me, like you decided that.". . . That's a hard process for a parent to put a child through, but at the end of the day, both of us acted like fools . . . in the courtroom and is only gonna lead to one thing. . . . The judge is still gonna say what . . . a lot of people need to understand like it's not the court's fault that you're here. . . . I try to fight for my child as much as I can the right way. . . . First and foremost, you have to be open ears and an open mind to absorb and to accept . . . follow protocol, go through all your proper venues. . . . You can even talk to the Legal Aid [defense attorney] . . . if you don't like what he's tellin', . . . you have the right to seek your own legal counsel and you have the right as long as you read the papers.

Reflecting on her experience where both she and her mother did not necessarily respect the court's authority and "acted like fools" while her own case progressed, Marsha now believes that it is up to the family to understand how to work with the court in the "right way," by which she means to become informed about the process and to respect the judge's ultimate authority over the youth. She challenges others to seek out information on their own.

> If the family has no understandin', then the child will have no understandin'. . . . Our parents, they were probably indignant about certain issues. . . . Parents don't understand if you don't break that cycle, your child is gonna be indignant to certain things and have prejudices. . . . People always [say], "Oh it's our culture. . . . Alright that's our culture . . . [but] we can learn and we can make it better. If you don't educate yourself, how you gonna educate someone else? . . . Once you get a set of papers from the courthouse, they take them, they look at the date, they throw them away. I read every set of lettering and article. Even if I don't understand, I take myself to the library. I research this law and this article or whatever the case

I have to read. . . . While you doing that, educate your child because maybe with this process of them doing wrong, you could turn it into a right way and you might enlighten their mind for doing legal research that maybe one day they might take the bar exam and become an actual lawyer.

Marsha could have viewed Malcolm's arrest as unfair and through a racialized lens of the court and school systems being unduly harsh and discriminatory toward him. That is, he brought the knife to school to show it to a girl who had previously stabbed him with a pencil; instead of seeing Malcolm as a victim in the prior incident, the school referred him to court on a delinquency charge. Meanwhile, the girl, whose race was not stated in the interview, somehow avoided getting arrested or a school punishment for her actions. However, Marsha characterizes that perspective more as an ungrounded form of indignation. Her own experience in the past leads her to take a different approach now to her son's case. She sees her son's court case as an opportunity for both of them to learn about the law and to "break the cycle."[5] Intergenerational involvement in an institution, then, does not necessarily lead to the same outcome, but rather, could help empower the family with knowledge to avert, mitigate, or change it.

Making Comparisons

The influence of families' past experiences on their current ones is more nuanced than just applying knowledge from them to a current experience. Families also make their own localized assessments of the similarity in situations from which to use that information. For example, parents might conflate experiences they had as children with those of their children, even if the circumstances may be slightly different. Talia discusses how her past institutional experiences related to her mental health issues shape and legitimate her actions regarding Samuel's court and school situations:

Talia said she has seven disabilities: two phobias (going outside, small spaces), bipolar disorder (BPD), obsessive compulsive disorder, ADD, manic depression with suicidal tendencies, and schizophrenia. She says she never heard voices or saw things. . . . When she was nine years old, a caseworker told her to say she was schizophrenic so she can get out of an abusive foster home. Now that diagnosis follows her around. She got diagnosed with BPD last year when Samuel got the court charges; she had to be evaluated as part of that. She said that if she really had all those diagnoses, how did they [child welfare] let her keep her four kids?

Talia discloses several mental health diagnoses to me while also saying she does not believe she has all of them. Lest one think Talia arrived on her own to this conclusion that she may not have all these diagnoses and that she can handle them on her own, she mentions past interactions with staff from different agencies that helped shape this view. She says a caseworker told her when she was a child to use the schizophrenic diagnosis to get out of foster care. She states in an interview that doctors affirmed her sense that she is doing well despite her diagnoses, saying, "They send multiple doctors out to evaluate me one time, and it was like, 'As a matter of fact, we think that you're phenomenal because of all of the things that you've been going through and you're still focused. You have never been in jail.' I'm like, wow, I felt so good. People had me thinking I was crazy." While these statements do not necessarily prove that the mental health professionals agree with her about not needing any treatment, what is important analytically is that she invokes these officials' words to validate her perspective about her illnesses.

Her view also is informed by her perception of the staff's understandings and responses to Samuel's illness as limited. Below is an excerpt from a home visit where she explains her disagreement with the court staff's diagnosis of her son's oppositional defiant disorder:

> She says she told Samuel that she knows what it is like to live with a mental illness and she can help him with it—even if he doesn't take medication—because she doesn't either. I ask what he got diagnosed with; she can't remember the name, but it sounds like oppositional defiant disorder. She says that is not what it is; he hears voices. She says the staff didn't see how he talks to refrigerators or once when he was on the couch and his eyes rolled to the back of his head, he started talking about white birds. She said to him, "Let me speak to my son" and a few moments later, Samuel started talking to her; he didn't remember what had happened. I asked if she told him what happened; she says he pretended like he did it as a joke, but she could tell he was embarrassed by what happened.

The fact that the court staff doesn't see what she sees leads Talia to take charge in Samuel's treatment. In the following interview excerpt, she expands more on how he should address his mental illness:

> Well, he definitely still is mental because he was mental to begin with. He hears things. But he's trying. . . . We just try to teach him; so me, I just say, "You know what? Don't be foolish and don't set fires. You know fires is dangerous. Get out my face." That's me. I'm not gonna keep on petting you 'cause they say you have mental challenges, 'cause I do, too, and I know that you understand English. So, understand."

In addition to encouraging her son to handle his mental health issues on his own, Talia's belief that she can manage her own mental health condition shapes her efforts in her son's treatment, including who to call and which type of program to attend. Here is a fieldnote excerpt from the same home visit, when I ask her how Samuel is doing in school:

> She says he's doing much better. . . . She says he has ADD but she refuses to put him on Ritalin even though they (school) have been trying to get her to do that. She says that it is all mental and she has the same thing. She insists he can work hard to focus on his own and now that he's been trying, his grades in English are better.

Whether subtle or possibly misdirected, the parents' use of past experiences can be significant in how it shapes their involvement in the youth's case and subsequent outcomes. Talia does not agree with the school or court staff's ideas for treating Samuel's mental health issues. She rejects the school's recommendation to put him on medication for his ADD. Similarly with the court, the diversion staff informed me that the psychiatrist diagnosed Samuel with ADD and oppositional defiant disorder, ruling out mood and learning disorders. The psychiatrist's recommendations were individual therapy and medication management; the diversion staff subsequently referred him to a hospital outpatient clinic that provided those services. However, according to the diversion counselor, Talia refused that idea and chose to have him go to another program that offered preventive treatment. The counselor told me that Talia's choice "messed up everything" because the program she chose was not intensive enough and replicated the services already provided by the diversion program. While the diversion staff eventually referred him to a program for the individualized treatment and medication that they believed he needed, he stopped attending it fairly soon afterward. Meanwhile, the immediate outcome is that Samuel did not get treated for his mental illness, which continues to place stress on the family dynamics inside the home.[6] That delay also leads Talia to have a disenchanted view of the courts as being ineffective. Samuel ends up getting arrested for robbery charges and is tried as an adult, since he is now older than the maximum age of juvenile court.

Families' assessments do not always enhance their ability to manage a member's institutional involvement or issue, especially when families assume similarities between instances that may not be considered as such by institutions. Sixty-year-old Lita Velez is diligent about taking her eleven-year-old adopted son, Peter, to tutoring three times a week. Peter is very energetic, always trying to get someone's attention; when he speaks, it sounds like he has a little lisp. Lita explains that Peter has to go to tutoring because he was deaf until he was three years old and has language delays as a result; she was so afraid that it would be a permanent state that she is doing all that she can to help him now. Her approach to handling Peter's educational issues also is informed by her own experience in school. She says in one interview that she had a learning disability that never was diagnosed when she was in school, so she does not want him to go through what she experienced:

> I've got a learning disability thanks to New York City [schools] because they never taught me better. . . . That's why I go with Peter back and forth, whatever I've got to do. . . . So he could learn how to read because I can't read but my mother didn't do nothing because she didn't know better. . . . But I know better because I already went through that. So, I take my son, whatever we've got to do.

In another interview, she says:

> I gotta deal with a lot but I want to deal with it [Peter's learning issues] because I don't want him to get the same thing I [had]. . . . She [the counselor] lowered it [speech therapy] down for once a week but I told her to put him back twice a week 'cause he needs to go twice a week. If he don't need it, I will say he don't need it. . . . The only thing that he got problem is the speech and the reading and the writing. He's in eighth grade. He needs to learn how to write, like dictate. He needs to do that. I don't want him to go through the same thing that I went through.

It is not clear that Peter's learning issues are the same as Lita's, which she does not clearly outline. Yet she equates their experiences in the sense that they both have trouble with reading and writing. She does not want his issues with literacy to become a long-term problem as in her case, where she cannot read. As a result of her past experience, Lita is very motivated to be involved in Peter's case, making the hour-long bus ride three times a week, engaging with the tutor to make sure she is the right fit for Peter, and fighting with the insurance company, which tries to stop covering it several months later.[7]

This unintended influence of past involvements becomes more apparent when one considers Rosa Garza's comparison of her own experience to her youth's situations. Rosa is a fifty-three-year-old Brazilian woman whose previous hospitalization informs her approach to her fifteen-year-old stepson, José, who has HIV and a heart condition. She has been on disability for the past several years after sustaining a work injury as a nurse; her husband works in a grocery store. During the interview, she describes the impact of her hospitalization on her efforts to get José to be more active in managing his own illness even though she had a different medical condition:

> *Rosa:* I have my own issues because I suffered from major depression before. And I was hospitalized because of that. . . . I was codependent of my children's father before and had to learn how to not to be. . . . Now I try to teach people. . . . Sometimes I say, "No, I can't come." I purposefully don't go to the visits with Dr. Lehigh [José's doctor].
>
> *Leslie:* In terms of the medicine, does José fill the prescriptions or do you fill them?
>
> *Rosa:* He goes. . . . I started preparing him. That's why me and Dr. Lehigh, sometimes we clashed because when he was walking to school, for example, "Why José is walking to school by himself?" Why? Why? 'Cause why not? The school is not that far from the house.
>
> *Leslie:* What was she [Dr. Lehigh] worried about?
>
> *Rosa:* I have no idea.

Rosa's experience with depression drives her need to foster José's independence both in terms of everyday life (e.g., walking to school) and his disease (e.g., going alone to the doctor, filling his prescriptions). That sometimes leads to conflict with José's doctor, who may not be aware of this connection of her past illness and her actions regarding José. This intergenerational involvement is not obvious in the sense that Rosa has a different illness than José. Yet it still shapes how she teaches her stepson how to interact with the doctor who also might see her actions as not helpful for José's illness.

While Lita's and Rosa's pasts make them more invested in their children's institutional involvements, it can have the opposite effect on other parents with their youths' situations. Sarah Roberts is a thirty-eight-year-old biracial woman whose sixteen-year-old son, Josh, is in juvenile court for assault against his dad. The court offered counseling for the family because Josh and his father were having problems. Her past experience with counseling makes her resistant to the idea, as she describes in her interview:

> *Sarah:* Me and his father were together for twenty-one years but we broke up for five years and his father was always in and out of jail, in and out his life, so when he came back in his life, he [Josh] wasn't ready for that but he tell him he can't come to my house and tell me what to do because you been out my life for five years, so you can't change me now, so that's where the disrespectful [behavior] came from. . . .
>
> *Leslie:* Did they offer you guys counseling at all?

Sarah: Yeah, they did . . . but I didn't want it and he didn't want it 'cause I didn't think we needed it and I didn't wanna talk to no counselors. . . .

Leslie: So, but did they make you do it?

Sarah: No.

Leslie: You didn't have to?

Sarah: It was a choice. . . .

Leslie: So, can I ask why you said no?

Sarah: I don't like talking counselor, it don't work from like when I was a little kid when I was molested and stuff. . . . I used to talk to them, but it used to make me madder and madder and madder and madder. It like, it don't do nothing for me.

Leslie: And your son also said he didn't want to do it.

Sarah: Yeah, he didn't wanna do it neither.

Leslie: And what about his father, did he have any ideas about that?

Sarah: He had ideas, but he didn't wanna do it either. None of us wanted to do it.

The mother and son's situations are different. Sarah's was about child molestation, and Josh's is focused on reducing conflict with his father, who is now living with them after several years apart. Yet her experience leads her to not encourage Josh or his father to consider therapy. Sarah does not mention if she told the court staff why she was resistant. If she hadn't, that might have prolonged the youth's case in two ways. One could imagine the staff seeing her rejection of therapy as an instance of her being "uninvolved" or "unsupportive" of the youth's needs. One could also imagine that if Josh and his father didn't manage to work out their issues, their conflicts could have continued or escalated, leading to further complications for Josh's case in court (e.g., if he got into another fight with his dad that leads to an additional "assault" arrest or acted out in other ways that violate his terms of probation).

Differing Perspectives

Parents' and youths' differing views of past issues can affect the extent and efficacy of the family's understanding as they lead to conflicting views about how to deal with their current institutional involvements. Consider this interview excerpt from Karen Williams, a thirty-six-year-old African American mother who is currently unemployed (she used to work as a security guard). Her twelve-year-old daughter, Savannah, has been dealing with weight issues since she was a baby. Karen discusses how Savannah and her different views of her sister's experience with obesity relate to their approaches to Savannah's condition:

> At one point she [Savannah] was like, "Oh mom, they have these pills on TV. Can you buy it for me?" . . . I said, "No, because you can do it yourself if you just stop [eating]. I'm not gonna buy you pills," because I have a sister that was really big, and my sister started taking these pills. She [Savannah] saw how my sister lost all this weight. That was great. If you see my sister now when she stopped taking those pills, she looks huger than she did the first time, so that's what I'm trying to explain to her.

Here, differing family views about a member's past illness can undermine the parental authority over the youth's illness work. Even though Karen thinks the main lesson to learn from her sister's weight loss experience is that she ultimately gained back the weight, she says Savannah only sees that the diet pills worked initially. The implications go beyond whether to use the pills; her aunt's weight loss could provide the evidence for Savannah that directly counters her mom's words about how to lose weight. That would empower her to ignore her mom's advice to eat smaller portions and exercise, advice that Savannah says in her interview the doctor mentioned to her as well. Instead Savannah also mentions in her interview that she manages her weight by skipping meals. Yet that does not help, as Karen reports that Savannah eats snacks secretly in the bathroom; she knows because she finds cake wrappers hidden behind the toilet. Seeing her aunt's approach may add legitimacy to Savannah's ideas about managing her weight, which ultimately are not effective.

The severity of a past issue does not reduce the possibility of different family member views, even in extreme fatal cases that could serve as a motivational "wake-up call" for everyone to pay more attention. Jessica King, a forty-five-year-old Caribbean American middle-class woman, discusses the asthma issues of her thirteen-year-old niece, Shannon, and sixteen-year-old nephew, Bryson. She became their legal guardian after their mother, her sister, passed away from breast cancer when Shannon was only four months old; their mother also suffered for years from severe asthma. Jessica is a supervisor in a city agency. She is warm, kind, and thoughtful as she talks; Shannon is slightly timid and soft-spoken, while Bryson is very polite with a dry sense of humor. Both Bryson and Shannon attend Catholic school and spend most of their spare time playing basketball for their school teams and other leagues. They live in a multi-unit family home in the Bronx with Jessica's parents (who own the house) and Jessica's twenty-nine-year-old daughter, Ashley, who does clerical work in a hospital. Shannon's father lives in a small unit in the back of the house. In addition to reminding them of what the doctors say, Jessica frequently brings up her sister's asthma and her frequent trips to the hospital emergency room at all hours, to underscore to Bryson and Shannon the importance of monitoring their asthma. She talks about Shannon in her initial interview:

> I don't think she quite understands . . . how serious it is and how she needs to—if she knows she's struggling breathing that she needs to let me know, that she needs to get on the [nebulizer] machine . . . even now that she's a little older and not to be so gross, but I would tell her, I said, "Your mom would make herself throw up so the mucus could come out. . . . Maybe you might need to do that."

Jessica is insistent that Shannon pay more attention to her asthma, particularly because she thinks Shannon often is unaware that she is wheezing to the point of needing the nebulizer machine.[8] Yet Shannon downplays the significance of her mom's experience and asserts confidence in her own ability to manage her asthma during one of my home visits:

> Shannon continues to say that Jessica worries too much—more than they [her brother and she] both do. Bryson isn't worried about his heart condition. And with Shannon's asthma, Jessica worries too much about that too. . . . I ask if Shannon can tell when she is not breathing normally. She says yes.

Shannon views her aunt's words as an expression of her personality as a "worrier" versus an indication of someone who has had experience seeing others manage the same kind of asthma. Even though she knows her mom often had to go to the emergency room when an asthma attack occurred, Shannon does not see the relevance for her own asthma. Furthermore, she doesn't seem to see the merit in Jessica's response to Bryson's newly diagnosed heart condition, dilated cardiomyopathy, even though his father died from the same condition several years ago. The disconnect between Jessica and Shannon's understanding about these illnesses becomes apparent in the following interaction during another home visit a month later:

> Jessica asks if Shannon is having trouble breathing. Shannon says no but Jessica says she can hear it. . . . Jessica puts her head on Shannon's chest [so

that her ear is right over Shannon's lungs]. She says she doesn't hear any wheezing. Jessica says the challenge with Shannon now is to figure out if she is having allergies or asthma. . . . Jessica says that Shannon's mom didn't have allergies so it's hard for her to tell the difference.

Shannon willingly allows Jessica to put her head on her chest but later expresses to me that she does not take it seriously. Despite understanding that her mom also had severe asthma, she views her aunt's actions as unnecessary. While Jessica does demonstrate a more sophisticated understanding of asthma, distinguishing between Shannon's symptoms that could be due to allergies versus her sister's case, Shannon reduces all of these actions to her aunt's worrying. In this way, whatever advantages Jessica's middle-class status might provide in managing the youths' health conditions do not translate to her niece and nephew's views or actions.

This section shows the complicated and nuanced ways that past involvement shapes a family's current institutional involvement. Whether legitimate or not, Talia perceives the mental health professionals as agreeing with her assessment of her own illness. That empowers her to take an active role in managing her son's treatment, including directing the type of treatment and agencies involved (e.g., calling juvenile court initially versus mental health organizations). At the same time, institutions might devalue parents' strategies that were based on their previous experiences with other institutions. For example, Rosa runs the risk of being seen as a negligent parent by the doctor and referred to child welfare for medical neglect like other families in this study. The intricacies of how past involvements affect the current case are important factors in families' navigation of the multi-institutional maze. They also present missed moments for staff to work more closely and effectively with families; if the staff knew more about these past involvements and how families view them as relevant for their current cases, perhaps they could have better understanding of parents' reactions to current institutional conditions, which would help them possibly even exit out of the maze more easily. Finally, it is important to recognize how individual family members recall the same past experience differently; those variations can lead to conflicting approaches to the current situation and potentially lead to tension between those members about their views.

INSTITUTIONAL VIEW OF PAST HISTORY

Institutions play a key role in the influence of family history on a case, both in how the staff interacts with families and views the families' past experiences. Cultural capital, or the resources, skills, knowledge, and background that a person has based on his membership in a particular social group, is a recurrent theme in this regard. The class advantage plays out in the court setting, as shown by Melissa's successful advocacy about her daughter's case that was discussed earlier in the chapter. Her middle-class cultural capital appears to work to her advantage here, as the court actors did not contradict or dismiss her claims. Similarly for some families dealing with health issues, middle-class parents used their knowledge of an illness gleaned from past experiences to legitimate their views in their interactions with the doctor.[9] Consider how a thirty-six-year-old middle-class biracial mom, Eartha Kiernan, discusses her experiences dealing with her fourteen-year-old daughter, Jojo, who has asthma. Eartha, an executive assistant at a local city agency, describes how she mentions the family history of asthma to the doctors when dealing with Jojo's somewhat ambiguous symptoms.

> She had a cold that wouldn't go away. . . . It was constant coughing. . . . We thought it was allergies. It wasn't that. And then she went to the doctor and I told him it runs in my family. My dad was very severely asthmatic. My brother's a severe asthmatic. So, I just told him to check. . . . They heard a little rattle, but it wasn't anything major. So, then they gave her the asthma medicine, the inhaler and the machine, and it seemed to help a lot.

Eartha uses her family history of severe asthma to legitimate two parts of this interaction. First it lends credibility to her decision to take Jojo to the doctor in the first place, as it "proves" her ability to distinguish the cough as separate from allergies. Secondly, she invokes her family history with asthma to validate her request to the doctor to check Jojo's cough and not dismiss it even when he didn't hear "anything major." The cultural health capital that Eartha has accumulated by seeing her father's and brother's asthma is evident here, not just in substance but also in how she harnesses the information to influence her encounter with the doctor.[10]

Even if the institutional actors have the best intentions, they often are not able to use family history effectively. The reason lies in two systemic factors: (1) how well the system actors get to know the families' own views of those histories and (2) how the systems are working with each other to help families or pass along families from one to another.

Two doctors' discussions of family history highlights the first factor. St. Simons, the hospital where they work, recognizes the importance of supporting families, assigning patient navigators to them to help manage the member's care. The doctors also take family health histories seriously and mention how they are trained to use motivational interviewing to get that information. In the following interview excerpt, Dr. Bhatia explains the significance of those histories:

> *Leslie:* Is there like a type of parent you find to be most supportive [of their youth's managing of the chronic illness]?
>
> *Dr. Bhatia:* Right. Um, I'm just trying to think about individual cases. . . . And that would be where there was a family scare.
>
> *Leslie:* Oh, okay, oh, interesting.
>
> *Dr. Bhatia:* Or a grandparent, you know, um, had a complication of diabetes.
>
> *Leslie:* Yeah, like they had a history, yeah.
>
> *Dr. Bhatia:* Or remember what happened to Auntie So-and-so kind of thing. . . . They have a personal experience with like a first-degree relative.

Dr. Bhatia suggests doctors see these "family scares" as a way to help encourage families given that they have had "personal experience," including those of extended kin, up close.[11] Yet the impact of those scares also depends upon how the families experience it. Consider how Dr. Peters tries to harness this family history in a meeting with the Hernandez family (who was featured in the prologue) about sixteen-year-old Gigi's diabetes. At this point, Gigi and her mother, Sulia, have not been actively checking Gigi's sugar levels, nor has she seen a doctor in several months. Dr. Peters is worried that they are not taking her diabetes seriously.[12] In the following interaction, Dr. Peters uses Gigi's grandfather's diabetes to encourage them to pay more attention to Gigi's condition. However, his efforts do not yield the expected results. The following fieldnote excerpt is a conversation between Dr. Peters and me before the family shows up, where he summarizes his goals for the meeting:

> Dr. Peters says that he called Sulia last week to discuss Gigi's test results. He says she has "poor control" over her diabetes and that today, he basically will have to "start again" with her and her mom about it. He says she hadn't been to the doctor in over a year when he first met her last fall and she doesn't appear to have gone back to see the endocrinologist regularly after the initial diagnosis in the fall. . . . He says her A1C result was 8.8. Before in September when she was first diagnosed, it was 8.6. That test measures the average glucose level over the past two to three months.[13] The other glucose test result was 194 (70–100 is normal).

Dr. Peters highlights the fact that Gigi is not keeping up with her doctor's appointments, both with him and with the endocrinologist at another hospital. He was more concerned about her not going to the specialist, where she would get regular blood tests and lessons on nutrition to help manage her diabetes. Gigi's latest abnormal results from two types of tests (A_1C and glucose) indicate to him that she and her family have not incorporated into their daily routine any of the information that the doctors gave them about diabetes. When Sulia and Gigi come, Dr. Peters first meets with Gigi alone before calling Sulia and me back into his office for the following conversation, as outlined in my fieldnotes:

> Dr. Peters is telling them [Gigi and Sulia] both that they are a team; if Gigi forgets, Sulia can fill in the details. Sulia says it is better for her to go to [the endocrinologist at] Dr. Peter's hospital so that Gigi can go on her own. He says you are a team though, suggesting that she go with her. He then asks Sulia if she knows anyone with diabetes. She says her dad. He asks if her dad is affected by it. She says it doesn't really affect him much except one time, he had low blood sugar and sometimes his legs are sore. Sulia tells Dr. Peters that the other doctors gave Gigi too much medicine and that it became almost like information in one ear and out the other. She doesn't explain much beyond that.

Dr. Peters asks Sulia about a family history of diabetes to help underline the importance of Gigi taking a more active approach to managing her diabetes. He asks after having first tried the "team" approach, to which Sulia does not appear to respond; she keeps the focus on Gigi, asking that her daughter switch endocrinologists to one at St. Simons where she could walk by herself. By asking if "her dad is affected by it," Dr. Peters tries to bring to the forefront the effects of what seems to be a slow-acting or invisible disease. However, Sulia views her dad's symptoms—sore legs and low blood sugar—as infrequent and not that serious. So, instead of this history helping drive home Dr. Peters's point about addressing the diabetes before it is too late, Sulia ignores it and redirects the conversation again to the other doctors, who overwhelmed her with so much information as to make it useless for Gigi and her.

Secondly, institutions need to do more than harness family history effectively while interacting with families; they have to have the capacity to address it. Ellen, a director of a court diversion program, talks in an interview about the systemic failures whereby the child welfare system passes on families' problems to the delinquency court:

> I think that like this would be easy to hear as like passing the buck, but it really strikes me that there are young people whose families have had ACS [child welfare] involvement since they were five or six [years old], and by the time they turn thirteen, now all of a sudden it's the criminal responsibility

of the young person, everything that's gone on. It's like there was no ACS involvement. There was no struggles . . . of the parent from before. But now ACS sort of passes it off and it's just as though we, as a society are saying, "Well, this young person keeps screwing up." Well, yeah, they're screwing up, but what were we doing for the last seven years? As a series of systems, what did we do?[14]

With its legal mandate to focus on the youth who is arrested for an offense, the delinquency court cannot sufficiently address the families' issues and previous institutional involvements, which in this case would be child welfare. Instead, its mandate is to focus on the youth's taking responsibility for his actions, as if those actions are independent of the past experiences. Yet while Ellen recognizes this inter-institutional conflict, the fact remains that the systems essentially individualize or compartmentalize the families' problems to the point where the families themselves become blamed for the systems' failures.

CONCLUSION

This chapter presents a multifaceted and nuanced view of the influence of family history on current cases as it looks at that history across institutions, both in intra- and intergenerational terms. To do so, it focuses on families' understanding of that history, versus the institutional actors' views or the case files' documentation of it. Sulia does not share the same sense about treating diabetes as Dr. Peters, whose view of her father's diabetes appears to be that it is much more serious than Sulia believes. As such, the chapter argues that the influence of that history cannot be fully captured simply by documenting the number of times that a family is involved in any one institution. Rather, it is important to capture the information from their involvement across institutions that families remember, use, and apply to other situations. Unless institutional actors take families' localized understandings into account, it will be difficult for them to use family histories effectively in processing the current cases.

Intergenerational poverty and race affect the temporal aspect of family institutional involvement, as many poor families of color talked about several members' experiences in the same institutions (particularly the justice and child welfare systems), suggesting their increased vulnerability to such interventions and surveillance. Yet, at the same time, this chapter does not take an overly deterministic perspective whereby lower-class or minority families would face a distinct disadvantage compared to middle- and upper-class or white families. Marsha's own personal experience as a youth in juvenile court has a greater impact on her approach to her son's current case than her general sense that there might be institutional racism in the justice system toward African Americans such as herself. Jessica's middle-class cultural health capital in monitoring Shannon's asthma doesn't transfer to Shannon's actions, as the latter has a different view about her mother's asthma (which Jessica invokes to compel Shannon to pay more attention to hers). Taking this kind of nuanced temporal view highlights the need to capture families' unique institutional histories to understand how they view or negotiate with their current multi-institutional involvements. To be clear, I do not dispute the likelihood that poor minority families will be more involved in institutions; in fact, it is more likely they could get stuck in the maze because their efforts are not validated as strongly as middle-class white families. What I am saying is that there are opportunities for agency for poor minority families—however slight—and unanticipated effects of past involvements for all families, regardless of race and class, that we need to consider more carefully in our attempts to understand how families experience and manage their institutional involvements and in many cases, get trapped in the multi-institutional maze.

CHAPTER 4

Who's in the Family?

Multihousehold Exploration of the Maze

Many of us can relate to the situation of dealing with institutional involvements for family members who live in different households, whether it is managing medical care for an elderly parent or shuttling between one's own doctor visit, a teacher-parent conference, and a child's therapy session. What is perhaps less tangible to grasp is how poverty shapes this process as unstable housing, health issues, and increased risk of justice involvement subject families to a fluidity of households that other families are less likely to experience. By *fluidity* of households, I refer to two different situations: one, where members in various households manage a person's institutional involvement, and two, where the makeup of the household might contain temporary stays that are unknown to the institutions.[1]

This chapter looks at the influence of that fluidity on the family's management of institutional obligations. It shows how household fluidity can lead to added or compromised opportunities in sharing resources (e.g., emotional and physical labor, material benefits, information exchange). This variation stems from two interrelated factors. First is the extent to which there is a shared agreement and understanding about the institutional obligations among all the family members involved in handling the cases. Second, the family members need to trust each other's willingness and ability to implement these obligations across different households. These factors become more apparent when considering families where the parents live in separate households and are dealing with their children's cases. In sum, the chapter shows how multi-institutional involvement works among families whose members may or may not reside in the same household. This becomes especially complicated when the lines of responsibility are not clear among the family members in that network, such as when the person listed on file is not living in the same household as the family or if the institutional task is harder to enforce when the person lives in multiple households.[2] In addition to affecting families' ability to navigate effectively through the maze, multihousehold institutional involvement also exposes the limitations to those institutions in adequately addressing these types of family situations.

FOUSKAS FAMILY

Eileen Fouskas is a forty-five-year-old white woman, slightly chubby, with thin blonde hair that she often wears in a high ponytail. She is missing a few teeth, which is very obvious as she often smiles when she talks; she is always friendly and bubbly when she sees me. Her two older sons, thirteen-year-old Patrick and twenty-two-year-old Joey, live with their father, Phil. Eileen has worked in childcare but has not had steady employment; she is currently on public assistance. Phil works in construction and spends hours away from home for work.

Eileen lives with her boyfriend, Ibrahim, and her youngest son, ten-year-old Brian, a short, skinny kid with thin spiky brown hair, in a rented two-bedroom basement apartment of a private house in Staten Island. The house has a gate and rock path leading to the driveway and detached garage. There is also a heated pool in the back, but Eileen and her family are not allowed to use it. It is in a mainly residential area, where it appears most people (not Eileen) have cars. While there are buses and the Staten Island train nearby, they take a long time to connect to other boroughs in New York City.[3]

Eileen has to interact with seventeen separate agencies for herself and her two younger sons related to education, mental health, juvenile court, public assistance, and child welfare. Having her children spread across two different households presents both opportunities and challenges for this family's institutional involvements. For example, Patrick has an open delinquency case in juvenile court that started while he was visiting Eileen in Staten Island one weekend; he was charged with arson after he and his friend allegedly threw a Molotov cocktail in a park toward a school. Managing the expectations for that case becomes complicated, as Patrick is now living full-time with his father in another borough, Brooklyn, which is at least one hour away by public transportation. Patrick's experience in juvenile court reveals the racial privilege experienced by white families that lessens to some extent their challenges in the maze. That is, Phil often leaves early for work and, according to Eileen, does not really supervise Patrick very closely to make sure he goes to school and his court-related appointments. Patrick does not go to school for weeks on end, triggering a child welfare case for educational neglect. Yet his court status remains unchanged, as the probation officer keeps giving him chance after chance. Patrick continues on probation with no additional arrests or violations. In comparison, the minority youth in my study who also had juvenile court cases did not get the same lenient responses, instead receiving probation violations for often less serious situations.[4] Yet as this chapter shows, it is not just Patrick's racial privilege that leads to that outcome, but also the multi-household family arrangement that enables him to fly under the radar of probation's and other institutions' surveillance.

ADDED OR COMPROMISED OPPORTUNITIES

The porousness of household boundaries can create both advantages and challenges for families in navigating the multi-institutional maze. For many families like Eileen's, the impact of such changing dynamics in the household is often a combination of both, leading to varying implications for their institutional involvement. This section looks at how these opportunities manifest across family members and households.

Increased Opportunities

Families find ways to use institutional rules to their advantage in dealing with family dynamics across multiple households. There could be three ways in which families see the benefits to this situation. One, the noncustodial parent could shift the responsibility of a child's institutional involvement onto the parent who has custody. Two, people could share information about their institutional involvements with their family members across different households, who would then benefit from that experience. Finally, families could avoid more institutional involvements by using the various households as additional resources.

Eileen's situation exemplifies the first two advantages. While Eileen and her ex, Phil, still are legally married, they have been separated for ten years.[5] By having custody of their thirteen-year-old son, Patrick, Phil avoids having to pay child support to Eileen. In some ways, Eileen sees the advantages to having Patrick live with his father. Having Patrick live with her is not good for her depression and anxiety; she repeats what her therapist said about her needing to take care of herself to be able to take care of others. The current arrangement helps her to stay calm, focus on her own issues, and take care of her younger son, Brian. She also uses the custody agreement to absolve herself of Patrick's court case, from doing the supervision to keeping his court-related appointments, as she tells me in the following fieldnote excerpt:

> Probation called today to see why Patrick was not in school and that they will need a conference soon. Phil said they will both go Tuesday. Eileen said no I am not the parent, you are and that she is not going to the appointment . . . [Five days later after the Probation meeting took place] Eileen said that Phil yelled terrible things at Patrick in the street beforehand (she heard it on the phone). He was cursing at him and threatened to move back to Greece, sending him back to live with her. Eileen said he couldn't move because "you've got custody."

In this case, the custody arrangements provide her with more influence on her ex, who currently is legally responsible for their middle son. She doesn't have much leverage over Phil in other ways, as he often drops Patrick off at her house without advance notice and chooses when to give extra financial support for their youngest son, Brian.[6] While Phil was probably not serious about his threat to move, Eileen's use of the custody arrangements points to how families can use institutional involvements to manage internal dynamics.

Information gleaned from institutional involvements also can be valuable resources for family members to share with each other. For example, Eileen is assisting her stepsister, Carla, and stepdad, John, with their cases, on top of dealing with her own institutional involvements. Besides advising Carla on how to receive housing assistance, welfare, and disability benefits for her son's ADHD, she also is helping John look for a new job and get his unemployment benefits:

> Eileen asks if John has his résumé. . . . I offer to look it over (after she suggests it). . . . Eileen did it for him. It has a lot of white space on it and things are laid out in a confusing way (under education, Eileen typed, high school with a typo, GED, college, but he only had a high school diploma). I ask him some questions to try to fill out the résumé some more and reformat it. When I go through it with him, he looks a little confused and then says Eileen will fix it for him. I ask if she has a computer here. She says no. She said she went to Workforce One to do it.

This excerpt shows how family members often share information with one another, regardless of whether they are living in the same household. Eileen has been on welfare for several years; it requires that she attend Workforce One, which provides job training and résumé writing. She can now share that information with John, who hasn't looked for a job in almost thirty years, as he worked for Sanitation during that time.[7]

Regarding the third and final advantage to multiple households, thirty-nine-year-old Maria Medina says that having her fifteen-year-old son, Carlos, spend time at his father's house not only helps her manage her current institutional obligations but also allows her to potentially avoid new ones. They recently moved from North Carolina to New York with Maria's husband (Carlos's stepfather) and her ten-year-old son (Carlos's half-brother). Maria claims Carlos's behavior was so bad at home and in school that she asked the court in North Carolina to place him in a group home. But after she had several medical procedures, she decided to move back to New York to be closer to family, as she grew up there. She recounts in her interview some past conversations with Carlos to highlight the conflicts that she faces:

> I can lose the other, the little one, because of what you doin' . . . and he said he don't care. . . . When we came here on March 12, we were living in street. But my baby father family took us inside, one bedroom 10 people [in] one bedroom . . . the next day he [Carlos] left to his [father's] family, not tellin' me where he's goin', nothin'. I said well I'm gonna pray he's gonna be safe. It was like a week; I found the number from his family and I called them and they told me that he's here. I say he did not tell me to give him permission or to go over there. . . . And I was like, you know, keep him over there because I'm gonna get my apartment, I am lookin' for [an] apartment.

Despite Carlos not informing her about where he was going, Maria can use his staying at the father's house to her advantage. It is more than just absolving herself from responsibility of his court case, like Eileen. Maria is able to take this time as a respite of sorts, to focus on a more immediate matter, such as getting her own apartment, and to avoid possible child welfare involvement for her younger child by not having Carlos misbehaving in her house.

Straining Resources and Added Stress

While multiple households can provide some opportunities to families, the same situation also can lead to difficulties in resolving some institutional cases. Phil is not supervising Patrick very closely, which leads to increased institutional involvement:

> Eileen says they got an ACS [child welfare] case that just started (the school initiated the referral after seeing hickeys on Patrick's neck and also seeing him hanging out after school on school grounds; she also says something about someone seeing him at McDonald's alone at 9 p.m.). She says they are trying to get the case closed. Patrick is basically being unsupervised at his dad's house—Phil works a lot and is never home. Her oldest son, Joey, tries to watch Patrick, but can't do it all the time. So now, they are trying to find someone to pick Patrick up from school and watch him until Phil gets home. . . . Part of the ACS case is about medical "neglect."

Eileen manages these involvements mainly on her own, even though she still sees Phil as the primary parent responsible for them. In addition to answering the staff's phone calls about Patrick's whereabouts (if she knows), she also has to manage Patrick's institutional obligations because of Phil's apparent nonexistent efforts to do so. That means she has to go back and forth on public transportation between three boroughs of New York City (e.g., Staten Island, Manhattan, and Brooklyn). When Patrick calls her to take him to his appointments at therapy, school, or probation, that entails a three-hour round-trip journey from Staten Island to Brooklyn for both Eileen and her youngest son, Brian, who she would have to bring along because she doesn't have childcare. If Eileen has to go into Manhattan to maintain her public assistance benefits, she might be less likely to agree to go with Patrick. This all contributes to her stress, as she has to manage these appointments and spend additional time getting to all of them.

> She said it's hard because Patrick doesn't want to ever go [to therapy for ADHD]. She also has to take Brian for therapy [also for ADHD]. Going back and forth from Staten Island to Brooklyn is a lot. Phil basically needs to get more involved because she can't do it alone. She said that Brian's old therapist used to only have daytime appointments so she would have to take him out of school early to get to his 3 p.m. appointment. The school would get mad about that. Now she found a new therapist who has evening hours (5 p.m.), which will make it easier. She says now she just has to figure out Patrick's therapy.

She has to balance one son's needs with her other son's need to see a therapist near her home. To further complicate matters, both sons' therapy is mandated by institutions: Patrick's from child welfare and Brian's from SSI.[8] If Eileen does not keep up with Brian's therapy, that will affect his SSI benefits, which cover much of her household expenses.

All of this places more of the burden on Eileen, further endangering her family's ability to stay in compliance for not just one but two institutions. It also leads to potential endangerment of income to her household (e.g., loss of Brian's SSI benefits).

This not only complicates the existing institutional involvements for the children but exacerbates previous issues for Eileen. Here is how Eileen describes the toll of these involvements on her during a home visit in mid-December:

> She says her days involve constantly running around; it never ends. She says if it is not one thing, it is another. She says Monday she had to go to ACS in Brooklyn to talk about Patrick not going to school or probation. Yesterday she had to take Brian to the therapist and then somewhere else to get his prescription refilled. . . . She says Patrick is stressing her out—she hasn't been able to go to her therapy sessions in a month. She finally called to schedule an appointment but now has to wait until mid-January to see her therapist (his next available opening). Normally, she goes to the therapist weekly and sees the psychiatrist once a month.

It is not just that the institutional involvements delay her own treatment; they also add to the need for that treatment, as the stress of Patrick's case affects her mental health. In mid-February, Eileen still has yet to see a therapist and mentions again to me at that point that she is feeling depressed. She eventually goes on a new anti-depression medication in late April.

Institutional Role in Creating These Opportunities for Families

Institutions affect how families are able to leverage effectively their multi-household involvements. As mentioned in the previous section, Eileen tried to help her stepfather, John, to find a job, based on what she learned from a workfare program. While that seemed to be helpful, she also notes the limitations of that knowledge in that the program only provided clients with a computer to type up their résumés, versus helping them search and prepare for job interviews. The poor quality of those services affects not just her case outcomes but also those of her family members such as John, with whom she shares her knowledge and resources.

Complications also arise in Eileen's family when multiple agencies do not appear to be coordinating with one another about a family member who spends time in different households. As stated earlier, Eileen's family has an open child welfare case for neglect due to Patrick's chronic truancy, which is largely due to his father not adequately supervising that his son goes to school. However, the child welfare agency apparently is not addressing the possibility that Phil, Patrick's dad, is verbally and physically abusive. Here is what Eileen shares with me during a home visit:

> Eileen says the dad [Phil] is not doing anything for Patrick. . . . Phil is yelling at him a lot and Eileen said he hits him too. She doesn't seem to be that concerned about it, simply telling Patrick to "keep his head down" and not to respond to his yelling so much. . . . Later, Patrick takes a second Cheez-it packet from the closet (Eileen hides snacks in there) and Eileen yells at him for doing that. She says she takes those when she goes to wait for appointments. Earlier she said though that Phil is not feeding him. He doesn't really give Patrick any money for food anymore. She is sending him home with peanut butter and jelly and mac and cheese.

When I talked with Eileen, she said the child welfare workers focused only on the school issues; they might not know about these other issues, as they mainly called her for updates about his school attendance. Eileen is not the only one to notice or hear about this alleged abuse: a diversion agency working with the court, Project CHOICE, told me that they called the child welfare agency to monitor the situation because of something Patrick had mentioned to them.[9] The director of Project CHOICE, Ellen, explained in an interview that "there was some concern regarding some statements Patrick made about his dad and about the way his—how he felt about the attention he got in the home. . . . We acted on the statements that he made and called state central registry." However, they did not hear any response about what happened. In addition, Ellen discusses the limited influence of her diversion program on the schools; she says, "We connected with the school a fair amount but after the superintendent suspension, your hands . . . start to get tied of what you can do to support the young person." This exemplifies yet another instance of institutional mismatch where there is an incompatibility of systems in which the diversion program and school had some inkling of a possible case of abuse but did not seem to know if the child welfare agency ever opened an investigation into the matter. Moreover, Ellen's agency tried to coordinate a response with the school, which did not reciprocate after Patrick got suspended for setting toilet paper on fire in the school bathroom. Meanwhile, Patrick continued to live with Phil for the entire time I did fieldwork with the family.

In addition, the institutions often do not effectively capitalize on the possibilities that are created by families living across households. For example, Eileen is struggling with the different rules in two agencies, welfare and FEGS (Federation Employment & Guidance Service), for her public assistance and workfare requirements.[10] Eileen's mom lives nearby with her husband, John, and can help her with childcare. But Eileen basically says FEGS is denying her application for her mother to provide the childcare, and without it, she cannot work or go to school, which is part of the requirements for welfare:

> She says she needs to call them [FEGS] on Friday to see if her application for her mom as childcare provider for Brian was approved. Her application has been denied three times so far. . . . She says that her mom was approved as the childcare provider for Brian before when Eileen worked as a babysitter in a day care when she moved out to Staten Island. I say it's weird then that it's not being approved now; she and her welfare case manager filled out the application together and fixed the parts that the FEGS people said were incomplete. FEGS gave her a list of approved providers; the problem is that none of them would pick Brian up from school to take him to the afterschool program.

She doesn't seem to understand why the paperwork for her mom to become Brian's childcare provider is denied repeatedly, especially since she was approved before. In addition, Eileen feels like it should be correct given she had help from another agency; similar to Leisy's housing case manager helping her with Kobe's SSI paperwork discussed in chapter 2, Eileen's welfare case manager helped her fill out the application for FEGS this time. However, without that childcare approval, she cannot go to work, given that the FEGS-approved list of providers will not pick him up from school. Her experience raises the question about how institutions could better recognize the few resources that poor families can access across households.

Temporary Living Arrangements

Temporary living arrangements also can complicate a family's institutional involvements by adding stress to members in the household. Ibrahim, Eileen's boyfriend of seven years, moved in after he got evicted from his apartment; it has been two years, even though his name is not on the official lease. She says he contributes about $400 a month toward the cable bill and groceries. While it seems that Ibrahim's presence has a positive financial impact on the household, it does have negative effects as well. The financial support he provides is tenuous, as he occasionally does not pay the cable bill (she recently had to cover half of one month's bill) or provide grocery support in a consistent manner. So even though he is the only one that has a full-time job in a car rental agency, Eileen still basically supports the entire household, with funds from child support, Brian's SSI, food stamps, and public assistance. In addition, Eileen talks about an incident with her boyfriend that explains her arm injury that occurred a few months before:

> She then says he [Ibrahim] pushes her around and tells me that is how she hurt her arm. She didn't fall, which is what she has been telling people. I ask if that is the first time he's hurt her; she says yeah, but when they fight, he has pushed her before. She says she won't take it anymore. Later she says that when she told him it is not working and that he should leave, he didn't take her seriously. I ask if she has anyone to talk to about this; she says she did talk to her brother about it and he said to come out [West to where he lives]. She says she'll go see in the summer if she likes it out there, but she doesn't want to make any rash decisions.

When I visited her a few months before, she said she fell while mopping the floor and fractured her arm. She had to go to physical therapy for that injury. Because she was still recovering from the fall and wasn't sure if she'd have to lift heavy stuff in classes, she didn't do the nursing class in early December, which would have fulfilled her workfare eligibility for public assistance. But not going to that class endangered her public assistance benefits. While Eileen ultimately did keep her benefits, her situation raises the possibility of other victims being doubly penalized if institutions misinterpret their signs of abuse as indications of "noncompliance" with their requirements, such as workfare.

Other families faced the tensions due to temporary living arrangements that often were unknown to the institutions working with them. The Velez family is one of those families. Fifteen-year-old Isabel Velez has been trying to deal with her weight issues over the past couple years. Isabel was diagnosed as obese two years ago and now has polycystic ovary syndrome (PCOS), a hormonal condition that affects women's menstrual cycle with potential impacts on their fertility. She is five feet, six inches, with long, curly, dark brown hair that she wears pulled up in a tight bun. Isabel is articulate, academically motivated, and mature. In the next two excerpts, she talks about her brother, Albert, who has been staying with his girlfriend, Amanda, in their apartment for two years; they sleep on an air mattress in the living room, which barely can fit a small sofa, dining table, and upright china cabinet. The apartment is fairly crowded with Isabel and her brother, Peter, sharing one room; their bedridden uncle, Martin, in another bedroom, and their parents, Juan and Lita, in the third one. While they do have two bathrooms, everyone uses the one in the hallway.[11] At one point, I count nine toothbrushes in a cup on the bathroom sink. In the following fieldnote excerpt, Isabel is sharing her frustrations about Albert with her mom, Lita:

> Isabel mentions Albert, her thirty-year-old brother, staying there with his partner on an air mattress [in the living room]. He edits commercials. Isabel doesn't think she needs to listen to him because he is not really her brother [biologically]. Lita says he is her brother and tells me that her mom raised her to respect her elders.[12] She understands Isabel's point of view but still. . . . Isabel gets more and more irritated (the tone in her voice gets more heated) as she recounts what happened this morning when Albert was being really loud [making it hard for her to sleep], but then asked her why she and Peter were not up yet for school [he didn't realize it was a school holiday].

A couple months later, she and her mother have a similar conversation after another run-in between Isabel and Albert:

> Isabel said Albert rules the house now, and it makes no sense if he doesn't pay any bills and it's her parents' house. She gives an example of how, before, her parents told her that neither she nor Peter could date, but now that Albert lives here, he said Peter could date. Now Peter has had girlfriends—he's in seventh grade. Isabel says it's not like she wants to date, but still. Isabel said earlier that Albert comes in her room and uses her stuff like her lotions and brush. . . . Isabel doesn't like Albert being there; she says he . . . should be more mature. . . . At some point, Isabel and Lita start arguing about how unfair it was for Albert to cut off the internet so abruptly. . . . Albert had a three-bedroom apartment for $700/month and lost it. Lita said he could have kept it so easily if he had just rented out two of those rooms to people. He said he didn't want to do so because he didn't want people in his house. Isabel says, "But now he can live here with other people?" Isabel says that Albert is "not smart."

We see in these excerpts how Isabel's conflicts with and about Albert—which might not be noted in the medical chart—only add to the ongoing stress on Isabel as she tries to deal with her weight. Isabel mentions three recent incidents in the past two weeks where she believes Albert oversteps his authority in the household: setting dating rules for Peter and her, using her stuff without permission, and also handling the internet account even if her mother pays for it. She is especially incensed about the last situation, as it means she is not able to use her phone to talk and text with friends over the Wi-Fi. These kinds of household pressures do not help her manage her weight issues. She describes one of her coping mechanisms to me during a visit a month later when I ask how she manages the up and downs. She says she thinks about eating—especially chocolate—to deal with downswings, but that the therapist told her not to do that.

At this point, it has been over two years since the doctors have mentioned her weight as an issue and four months since they diagnosed Isabel as morbidly obese. I go with Isabel and Lita around the same time to a follow-up medical appointment where they find out that Isabel has gained a little more weight and is now at 299 pounds. The doctor also points to some dark circles around her neck as indications of prediabetes. Isabel is supposed to take Metformin twice a day but often forgets. Even though her therapist is aware of her urge to eat as a coping mechanism, it is not clear if Isabel shares her frustration about Albert with the therapist or her doctors. Therapists and doctors can only deal with the information given to them, and the stressors stemming from uncertain living situations in families' lives can be difficult to capture and incorporate into whatever recommendations they provide.

FACTORS SHAPING THE INFLUENCE OF HOUSEHOLD FLUIDITY

Family members have to trust each other regarding their roles and ability in managing their institutional involvements across households. This section looks at those factors in terms of the information and responsibilities being distributed across the family members, including parents who are former romantic partners and are both involved in their children's institutional obligations. It considers the particular challenges that arise when those members are distributed across households, with some moving in between the households (e.g., youths going back and forth between their separated parents' homes).

Use of Shared Knowledge

Even if the person's knowledge could be helpful in another family member's situation, it also requires that member to listen. While Eileen's stepsister, Carla, appears to listen to everything Eileen says about applying to various agencies for assistance, she doesn't always follow through with what Eileen advises.

> Eileen says the reason she is so on top of Brian's health appointments and medication is that SSI will check up on her to see if he has been going; every three years, he needs to get reevaluated for eligibility. . . . She says her stepsister wants to get it for Richard [her son] but Eileen said she doesn't take Richard

to the therapist. Eileen keeps telling her to do it, but the sister isn't so consistent. . . . Eileen said later that her sister asks her about every single thing.

Similarly, Lita has extensive interactions with medical institutions for several health problems, many of which her family members have. However, her son, Albert, and the mother of his seven-year-old son, Charlie, do not listen to her, which partially leads to their son's recent hospitalization. Consider this interview excerpt:

> *Lita:* Charlie was here and I saw him and he was like pale and this here [his lips were] like kind of burgundy. . . . They're kind of brown. . . . I'm saying, so Albert, that kid is anemic. I think his blood count is low. So, his mother will check him.
>
> *Leslie:* Did she? You don't know?
>
> *Lita:* No. I don't know. But Monday they had to put him on blood transfusion.
>
> *Leslie:* What? That's pretty serious, right?
>
> *Lita:* It was serious. So, I told them [his mom and dad]. They don't listen to me. I said that kid has anemia, and you know he's always been with anemia and you gotta go check him 'cause I think his blood count's low.

Lita spends a lot of time dealing with family members' illnesses, for those who live inside and outside her house. Within the household, Lita oversees the home health aides for her brother, Martin, who is bedridden after being a gunshot victim twenty years ago, and also spends three afternoons a week taking her son, Peter, who has ADHD and learning disabilities, to tutoring and counseling. Outside of the household, Lita is dealing with her sister, who recently almost died from a brain aneurysm, and her husband's mother from Puerto Rico, who has a potentially life-threatening illness. Her grandson, Charlie, is often over at the house, even though he lives with his mom in a nearby apartment. Lita, who also suffers from anemia, noticed his lips were not the right color, which she said was a symptom of the anemia. While she is not officially responsible for Charlie's health, she does give advice to his parents, telling them to monitor it more closely. Yet her advice is ignored. This not only affects Charlie's care but also other family members' health issues: because she feels like no one listens to her, she leaves them to manage their health issues on their own, including Isabel's obesity. She says in the same interview about Isabel and Peter:

> *Lita:* She [Isabel] haven't drink those medicines for kinda a while.[13] And tomorrow, I just bought her the other bottle. Look. She still got two

bottles there because they only a little—she don't hardly drink 'em. But kinda I mean, I tell her I can't force you to do it, 'cause you're a big girl. But you know that that's your problem. I mean, it's my problem. I even tell her you're gonna get me in trouble because supposedly I'm your mom and you're supposed to listen to me. You don't listen to me, I don't know.

Leslie: What do you mean by getting you in trouble? Trouble with who?

Lita: They're [Isabel and Peter] overweight. You could get in trouble when they're overweight.

Leslie: With the doctors?

Lita: With ACS [for medical neglect]. . . . I think I heard somebody do it once.

Leslie: Oh, where they could come in and do something?

Lita: And take them. I said okay, fine. Good, great. They get mad when I say that. Okay, good great. They can come and take you guys. I only joke with them like that.

Her insight being ignored in one situation leads her to withhold it from another situation (e.g., Isabel and Peter's health) that perhaps needs it just as much, if not more. She then jokes about ACS threatening to take them out of the home. While this threat of ACS that is disproportionately used on minority and poor families appears internalized in Lita's parenting, it does not have the intended effect. That is, it does not work to encourage the parent or children to be more compliant with the institutional rules (e.g., Isabel taking her medicine) but rather, serves as a halfhearted attempt at humor on Lita's part that only upsets the children who take the threat seriously.

Trust in Shared Responsibility across Households

In addition to sharing information with one another, family members share the responsibility in managing institutional tasks, even if the institution primarily holds only one or two responsible (e.g., the parent and/or the youth) for those tasks. In some ways, this situation could benefit the family when multiple households work together on the task. Yet there is one contingency that enables a family to see this multihousehold management as an advantage: the members need to trust the person to be responsible to take care of the task and that person. For example, as discussed earlier in the chapter, Eileen cannot resolve Patrick's ACS case because she cannot rely on her ex, Phil, to manage those appointments.

Several families described one unintended consequence of having youths spend time with family members across households: parents feel they are being blamed for situations that are not completely in their control due to this movement. Consider Sasha Johnson, a thirty-nine-year-old African American whose seventeen-year-old obese son, Tyrone, is currently living with her mother during the week. He stays there so he can attend a better school closer to her mother's home. But having Tyrone in a better school has serious consequences for his health in that his grandmother is not effective in managing his weight issues. While Sasha tells her mother what not to cook for him, she also understands where her mother's resistance is coming from, saying in her interview:

> It's hard to tell your mom, "Don't give your [grand]son this and that," 'cause you'll get the backlash, you know? . . . She's like, "I used to feed you like that." I said, "I understand, but these is different times, Mom." When they're old fashioned, it's hard to sink into their head you cannot give kids certain things. You remember when we used to go to school? It never had none of this, the nutrition facts, remember?

Sasha does eventually convince her mom to start baking instead of frying food and to give salads instead of coleslaw to Tyrone. However, she recognizes it is easier for Tyrone to continue unhealthy eating habits at his grandmother's house since she goes to bed so much earlier than him:

> He'll sneak out the soda that he sees she has on the bottom [of the refrigerator]. She even hides her soda, so when the morning comes, she'll say, "Wait. This soda was here when I went to sleep. Who drunk it?" Him, in the middle of the night, so I told her ease off the soda. If she's giving him a soda, hide it. He probably could get a soda once a week, but he used to sneak them and went and drank them at night.

Again, even if these family members are all supportive, the extent to which parents can control the situation varies. One can see how parents have to decide sometimes between equally important priorities for their children: health or education. Being a "good" parent in one institution (focusing on Tyrone's education) means risking being seen as a "bad" parent in another (not adequately supervising his food intake and weight).

The Ex-Factor

The impact of these issues (e.g., shared information, trust, and tasks across households) on a family's navigation in the maze becomes most apparent when considering people who no longer are together romantically but continue to coparent their children. While not all former partners have greater difficulties in managing institutional obligations compared to parents who live together, there can be more challenges for the former, especially if there are disagreements or a lack of coordination of actions across the different households in which they reside. In these situations, the institutional pressures become magnified in three ways: (1) parents' reconciling the actual work of the institutional involvements amid the organizational account of the "parent on record" (2) parents disagreeing about the treatment plans and (3) the prospect of more institutional interventions affecting the kind of help provided by the noncustodial parent.

Multiple households among exes raise a challenge when the official parent on record is not the one who manages the institutional responsibilities or the institution does not recognize the parent as having the authority over the youth (e.g., stepfather with no official custody). This division adds to the already daunting task of staying in compliance with institutional obligations, delaying or complicating the possible resolution of the case and keeping families stuck in the multi-institutional maze. Eileen Fouskas's family epitomizes how the difficulties in dealing with exes and institutions are more complicated to resolve than just simply changing the parent on record. As discussed earlier in this chapter, Eileen has to stay involved with Patrick's institutional obligations even though Phil is the custodial parent, as the staff from multiple institutions (e.g., school, probation, mental health agency) call her to ask about Patrick. Yet there is only so much she can control or know regarding his actions or whereabouts because she is physically not living with Patrick. She often tells the staff the little she knows, suggesting that they contact Phil for a more detailed update because he has physical custody of Patrick. However, Phil leaves early for work and does not answer his phone when they call. That leads to two types of child welfare cases: one for medical neglect and another case for educational neglect as Patrick is not going to school.

While it appears the parents (or more specifically, the father) are responsible for this lack of oversight, it is also important to note how institutions create this situation as well. Patrick's court case originated in Staten Island but was transferred after a while to Brooklyn, where he lives with his father. As a result, the agencies in Staten Island that started working with Patrick would have difficulties in continuing to do so since he lived too far away to fulfill their requirements. For example, the court diversion program (CHOICE) could not require Patrick to attend its afterschool programs once he moved to Brooklyn because of the time it would take for him to travel there after school; it also did not have the staff to check on him in Brooklyn.[14] As such, they marked him "compliant" with the understanding that they had a limited mandate over him. This also affects how much the institutions can get to know the families' issues because they are all only working with part of the picture. These geographical limitations allowed Patrick to essentially fly under the radar of his father, mother, and institutional staff. Patrick stopped going to high school but somehow avoided getting in trouble for it, even though he eventually accumulated almost eight months of absences during the year that I did fieldwork with this family.

Angelica Romero, a thirty-five-year-old Latina, also discussed in her interview the challenges in having the father of her seventeen-year-old daughter, Layla, have legal custody. For Angelica, it affects her attempts to take her daughter to the doctor, as the dad is listed as the parent on record:

> *Leslie:* So, do your other children go to the same clinic as Layla?
>
> *Angelica:* No. Since Layla lived with her aunt and her dad, they had a different clinic. So, when my son has to go to the pediatrician—so when I came over with Alma [her other daughter], we sent Alma to my son's pediatrician. So, for Layla, we have to do a transfer to switch her over to the other kids' pediatrician. . . . Her dad—since he still has custody over her—he had to do that with her because he's the one registered there in the papers.
>
> *Leslie:* In order for Layla to be in the same clinic, her dad is the one that has to make the transfer—transfer her?
>
> *Angelica:* Yes.

Layla came from the Dominican Republic to live in the United States with her father to receive better medical care for her asthma. Angelica only recently came to the United States from the Dominican Republic with her daughter, Alma, to rejoin her new husband and son. Yet she is now the one managing all three of her children's doctor appointments. While this instance seems not so serious and can be easily resolved once Layla's father completes the paperwork to transfer doctors, it does point to potential challenges for other families if the parents are not as cooperative with one another or the institutional issue is more acute.

Continuing in that vein, families can become more entangled in institutions if the parents disagree about how to manage the institutional obligations. These conflicts subsequently complicate how they interact with other institutions. It adds stress on the custodial parent (who in my sample, was primarily the mother) who has to manage the child's issues and interact with staff across social control institutions. When I first met the Wilsons, a Caribbean family, the mother, Michelle, was forty-one-years old; her daughter, Shakera, was fourteen years old and her son, Kevin, was two years old. They lived in a three-bedroom, one-bathroom apartment in the Bronx. Michelle is short and fairly fit, while her daughter is much taller and bulkier. Michelle was trying to get Shakera placed in a youth group home due to her disobedience with curfew and problematic school attendance. During the twenty-one months that I was doing fieldwork with the family, Michelle was working with both child welfare and the juvenile court staff, who now agree that the only viable option is placement. Yet Shakera's father, Kwame, is not cooperating, as noted in this extended excerpt from a home visit.

> Michelle tells me she is filing for a PINS [person in need of supervision] in family court on Monday. She tried to do it before when Shakera was 13 but the court didn't think it was appropriate at that point. So, they referred her to ACS [child welfare] to work with the family first, having her and Shakera go to therapy. Shakera did that for four months but stopped. ACS closed the case. It told Michelle that she would have to wait three months before it would reopen the case, which ended up happening. She says she feels like she is getting the runaround while seeking help and Shakera is just getting worse. They (ACS) did an elevated risk assessment. . . . Now they say it is time for PINS.
>
> Michelle says this is not normal teenage behavior, her coming back at all hours and not listening to her mom at all. Shakera is just openly disobeying her mom. Her dad also is not taking responsibility for her; he doesn't want her institutionalized but at the same time, won't take her into his home. . . . I then ask her for clarification about how Shakera ended up going to the hospital. Michelle says she called the cops. . . . They took her to the hospital for a psychiatric evaluation. The hospital threatened to call ACS for neglect if she doesn't come pick her up. . . . Kwame ended up picking her up and was supposed to take her to his house, but he brought her right back to Michelle's home, ringing the bell from downstairs. . . . She mentions that her mistake the last time [Shakera was hospitalized] was not sending Shakera upstate to the place that the hospital recommended. . . . She should have done that, but Kwame said no.

On the one hand, one could view Michelle as an ineffective mother trying unsuccessfully to set limits for Shakera, with her idea to call the police and to leave her daughter in the hospital to facilitate an ACS placement in a group home. Yet in the excerpt below where Michelle explains what led up to that point, we can also see how both Kwame and social control institutions have stymied her efforts:

Michelle says that Shakera pushed her. She said she would hit Shakera before she lets Shakera hit her. Since she knows she can't do that, she is trying to get help before it gets to that point. Shakera was trying to go out the window and also saying she'd run away. Michelle says it was really bad.

Michelle mentions at least two times that Kwame interfered with her intent to help their daughter (e.g., denying Michelle's wish to put her in placement during the first hospitalization), while also not taking any of the responsibility in managing the situation (e.g., picking her up from the hospital the second time but not taking her into his home). It is not just a matter of disagreeing parents; rather this conflict is further shaped by the fact that Kwame has another house, which the institutions can consider in their decisions about where to send her. That left Michelle to deal with Shakera, who she insists is becoming more disobedient and reckless. Michelle's family is drawn deeper into the multi-institutional maze that gets more complicated, with each turn becoming a detour to another. The court and ACS initially didn't think Shakera's disobedience was a serious problem that merited placement. Meanwhile Michelle has to take care of her toddler son, who has serious asthma problems of his own, as well as her own health issues. It takes three years and three hospitalizations that she told me about (including one not mentioned above) to place her daughter in a group home a few months after this latest incident.[15]

Finally, parents mentioned the possibility of institutional interventions affecting the financial, logistical, or emotional support from their exes. One fifty-four-year-old African American mother, Angela Scott, did not tell her ex-husband about the court case for their sixteen-year-old son, Jason, after he was arrested in school, because she was afraid about potential custody issues. Even though she does want her ex's support in dealing with the son, she said in an interview, "I think his father don't know about it [the case]. 'Cause if I tell his father, . . . they will try to take him from me." In addition to dealing with the logistics of the court case (e.g., finding/paying for a private lawyer and dealing with the court requirements), the stress generated from the court case is augmented by the fear of her ex using it against her in regard to custody. All of this limits Angela's response to help Jason resolve his court case.

CONCLUSION

This chapter extends how we conceptualize family involvement to include temporary living situations or members living across multiple households. It shows the challenges in how families manage and institutions accommodate these types of living situations. On the one hand, families have added opportunities by having extra members to help them navigate their institutional involvements. This situation offers a more optimistic view of family support, as more people could share information and tasks. Poor families also can use these situations for their own purposes, such as managing their relationships by invoking the institutional rules. It is important to recognize those opportunities and moments that might otherwise go ignored to discover glimpses of agency for the families.

At the same time, the chapter has shown the conditions under which the fluidity of households only complicates and, in some cases, worsens the family's management of its institutional involvements and the institutional responses to family situations. That is, it could be compromising if parents cannot trust their family members to help with the issue (e.g., Sasha's mother monitoring Tyrone's eating or a former couple like Michelle and Kwame not agreeing about how to deal with their child, Shakera). If institutions do not know of temporary living situations, it could affect the efficacy of the treatment (e.g., the added stressor on Isabel's weight management of Albert and Amanda living in Isabel's house). Finally, families may find institutional responses become limited if the issues they face cross households; these situations are exemplified best by families with parents in two different households (e.g., Eileen and Phil managing Patrick's probation, school, and child welfare cases).

More broadly, this multihousehold involvement reveals the ways in which socioeconomic status shapes a family's navigation through the multi-institutional maze. On the one hand, the framework of understanding how families share and use information, as well as their trust in each other to administer the tasks across various households, could be applied to situations of families from all socioeconomic statuses. One could imagine a family with divorced or separated middle-class parents who face the same challenges in navigating a child's medical or school issue if they do not agree on the approach to dealing with the situation or fail to coordinate efforts across their multiple households. On the other hand, poor families face additional burdens, as their socioeconomic status often leads to a fluidity in household makeup that is not within their control or known to the institutions working with them. That fluidity complicates the families' institutional involvements as their resources get stretched even further and institutions also may not be flexible enough in their requirements (e.g., parent on record) to reflect these families' movements across households.

CHAPTER 5

Mitigating Factors

Institutional Mismatch and
Unpredictability in the Maze

Understanding the family's navigation through the multi-institutional maze, as shaped by its concurrent, past, and multihousehold involvements, is complicated enough. While mentioned briefly in previous chapters, mental health issues, domestic abuse, and immigration are discussed in greater detail in this chapter as factors that further shape how families experience and go through the multi-institutional maze. In particular, this chapter shows how these factors expose the instances and implications of institutional mismatch in the maze.[1] Institutional mismatch refers to situations where the institutions' services do not fully respond to the family's issues, and yet they continue to work with them in some capacity, either by the family or institutions' initiative. The partial response by one institution often leads to the family's involvements in other institutions, which equally are unable to fully resolve the family's needs. These contingencies, or mitigating factors, also highlight the unpredictability in the maze, given that the same institutions could be either helpful or punitive toward the family regarding the same problem.

Mental health issues are perhaps the most prevalent among the three, with almost half the families (44%) saying at least one member living in the household had depression, anxiety, schizophrenia, or ADHD, and more than a quarter of them (28%) reported two or more members did. This chapter will explore how parents and youths navigate multiple systems for treatment when the issues go beyond one household; it also will look at how mental health issues affect families' institutional involvements and vice versa. While less common, domestic abuse—both intimate partner violence and child abuse—highlights in even greater detail the insufficient and incompatible responses from institutions in working with families to address that abuse. Finally, two facets to immigrant families' lives in the U.S. shape the unpredictability and institutional mismatch in their journeys in the multi-institutional maze: cultural conflicts between parents and youths and institutional involvements that span borders.

BRYANT FAMILY: MENTAL HEALTH
AND DOMESTIC ABUSE

The Bryant family lives in a small three-bedroom, one-bathroom apartment on the second floor of a small two-story building right in front of a bus stop in a working-class neighborhood in Staten Island. The building is on a commercial street with small businesses (e.g., dry cleaners, pizzeria, a check cashing place, a barber, and delis). The apartment opens into a living room filled with couches, a small TV, and pictures of the children on the walls. The bathroom and kitchen are to the right of the living room. Two bedrooms are on the left side of the living room and the third is in between the living room and kitchen.

The head of the household, Catherine, is a fifty-one-year-old African American woman who speaks with a gravelly voice, coughing occasionally, and walks with a cane due to her arthritis. She is medium height and has short-cropped hair; she doesn't wear much makeup and wears casual clothing such as oversized T-shirts, sweatshirts, and jeans. When I first started fieldwork, Catherine was living with her two grandsons, Edward (thirteen years old) and Shawn (fifteen years old), along with her nephew, Rodney (five years old). The boys are all skinny; Edward looks much younger than his age due to his short height and baby face.

Almost every facet of the Bryant family's life is open to institutional purview. They currently are involved in eleven institutions: a hospital, court, child welfare, disability, HIV/AIDS agency, public assistance, mental health agency, school, Medicaid, a drug treatment program, and church. These institutions do not always work in conjunction with one another, making Catherine feel like she cannot appease them all. Her rent is primarily paid for by the HIV/AIDS Services (HASA); she is HIV positive, but her levels are undetectable. HASA would like her to move out of her apartment because the stairs are hard on her arthritic knees. However, she wants to stay in that apartment, mainly due to Edward's legal troubles. She says in an interview, "We are the only ones in the building, and I like it like that . . . because Edward's got a problem with stealing a lot, so I don't want something to be missing down on the neighbor's house when it comes to Edward." Meanwhile her health becomes even more precarious as her knees make it hard for her to go up and down the one flight of stairs to her apartment.

Catherine's multiple institutional involvements also shape her decision about how much to work. Shortly after I started fieldwork with her family, Catherine started working as an HIV outreach counselor. While her employer keeps sending her to more trainings and increases her hours, that does not necessarily mean she will have a salary or benefits. So even though Catherine wants to develop her job skills and work more, she is hesitant to do so, due to her belief (whether true or not) that the benefits she gets from HASA and Medicaid may be curtailed and essentially not covered by the new job.

The number of people living in the apartment fluctuates at any given time, partly due to their institutional involvements. Over the course of the year that I conducted fieldwork, seven additional family members lived in the apartment at various points: five of Catherine's grandchildren, her daughter, and her daughter's boyfriend. Two of Catherine's granddaughters moved in after she opened a PINS (Persons in Need of Supervision) case in juvenile court against Shawn when she suspected him of starting to use marijuana and staying out all night. Catherine ultimately decided to send Shawn to live with his mother down south. Catherine's thirty-six-year-old daughter, Tanisha, her thirty-four-year-old boyfriend and their one-year-old baby came to stay after being evicted from their apartment; they stayed in Edward's room after he was arrested and placed in detention. While Shawn and Edward were no longer living in the apartment, Catherine and Rodney were there the entire time; at one point, eight people lived in the house with three bedrooms and one bathroom. This fluidity of household makeup not only presents an inconvenience to Catherine, but also affects her institutional involvements because Catherine faces a dilemma of notifying the institutions of the new household members. For example, because her rental assistance is based on who is staying in the house, her rent goes up when she takes Edward and Shawn off the list. While she could just add her daughter's family to that list to decrease her rent, she does not want them to stay long term, partly due to three issues potentially leading to institutional interventions: (1) Rodney's erratic behavior in school that Catherine views as a reaction to the number of people in the house; (2) the increased water usage and wear and tear on the apartment due to the new household members, which Catherine worries will affect her relationship with the landlord; and (3) Catherine's high blood pressure, which is elevated due to the higher levels of stress related to her daughter being there.

This brief overview provides just a glimpse of how difficult it is to parse out the Bryant family's institutional involvements due to competing institutional rules and the changing number of members in the household. Mental health and domestic abuse issues further complicate that process, as they further complicate the Bryants' journey in the maze, to which we now turn.

MENTAL HEALTH

Mental health issues can redirect a family's journey through the multi-institutional maze in two ways. First, institutional involvements might affect family members' mental health and vice versa. Second, it is difficult to manage a family member's mental health issues across households. Catherine's family exemplifies the first issue, as its past institutional involvements have left lingering impacts on various members that shape their internal dynamics. Below, Catherine is describing in an interview the ongoing trauma of her arrest while living in public housing:

> Before I moved here, his [Edward's] father and them got me arrested. His father and my other son had marijuana in my house. Me and my five-year-old [Rodney] just walked in the door, and they [the police] kicked the door in. . . . That's how I lost my apartment. I was living in city housing, and they found a pound and a half of weed. . . . I got over because like they said I just had came home, and the warrant was in my name, but that's—it had two names on it, and my son didn't live there. . . . Unfortunately, one strike, you're out in housing. . . . That's why I don't let my sons even come in my house. . . . It happened, what, two years [ago]? Yeah, two years, and I still have nightmares about me being locked up. . . . And it made my health worse, because I already had arthritis and was laying on that bench [in the jail for three days] in the damp and cold. They said it went into my spine now.

In a subsequent home visit, Catherine adds that the police thought initially that she was the head of the drug ring and that Tanisha, her daughter, used her tax refund of $2,500 to bail her out. Even though the charges were dropped a few months later due to lack of evidence, the impact of it affected the family's other institutional involvements. First, they did not get the bail money back for a long time. Secondly, the public housing authority ended up evicting Catherine; it said Eric (Edward's uncle) should not have been there, since he was arrested for drugs before. Catherine said she could have appealed but did not want to do so. Meanwhile, she recounts in an interview how she follows the advice from the judge during that time to this day; this advice shapes her current relationship with her two sons now:

> Catherine: She [the judge] told me, she said, "Leave your kids. That's the only thing I have to say to you. They're grown. They can do it on their own," and from that day, I listened to what she said. My son would be ringing the bell. I said, "You know I gotta search you." "I ain't coming up there." "Well, then, don't come up, because I never know if they're following you all." No, I'm not jeopardizing myself again.

> Leslie: But you still like see them outside of the house?

> Catherine: Yeah, I see them outside. I won't get in the car with them [laughs]. . . . I told 'em, "I really do have nightmares," and then the five-year-old [Rodney] had to stay with my other son while I was locked up, and he said, "Well, my mommy don't love me no more. She's not coming to get me." He thought I just left him, so that was tough. . . . He told the whole school. . . . "My mommy got locked up. The cops had her handcuffed," so everybody knew about it [laughs]. I was so embarrassed.

She also mentions the effects of this incident for herself, her relationship with her sons and also her nephew, Rodney, who calls her Mom. She and he were both traumatized by this arrest. So even if the arrest and jail stay were only for a few days, the incident had a lasting impact on her to the point where she still has nightmares and refuses to let her sons into her new apartment. The incident also affected Rodney's schooling, if only in how he expresses fear of abandonment to his classmates and teachers, who now know of Catherine's arrest, which leaves her so "embarrassed."[2]

Families face other challenges regarding mental health and multi-institutional involvement. For one, a family's concurrent involvements with non-mental-health institutional actors can facilitate or impede the person's mental health treatment. This highlights the unpredictable character of the multi-institutional maze in that the families' access to mental health treatment depends on which agencies they ask for help, as well as how those agencies respond to them. Families could then get further entrenched in the maze, without necessarily getting the services for the youth's mental health condition. For example, Catherine gets caught in institutional crosshairs as she deals with Rodney and Edward's ADHD. Rodney's school is monitoring his ADHD, which

Catherine says has a negative impact on Rodney, as she and Tanisha explain to me during a home visit:

> We talk about Rodney's meds. Catherine doesn't give it to him on weekends or after school even though it's supposed to help with homework. She says he is fine doing the homework as is. On weekends, he's fine without it. When he is on the meds, he doesn't want to eat and is spaced out. He's not Rodney, Tanisha says. Catherine says that's what the school wants—for him to be medicated. This morning she saw his two pills on the bed (he usually takes it by himself) so she went back to the school to give it to him. She knew the teacher would call her to ask for them. But Catherine is going to have to monitor him taking it now because she found a pill on the floor, which is a problem with the baby in the house (she doesn't want the baby, Tanisha's daughter, to eat it by mistake and then child welfare might come back in). Catherine says that what she doesn't like about the medication is that Rodney internalizes it to believe he is dumb without meds. He said the teacher told him that. Catherine told the teacher about that and the teacher clarified what she said; she said he was restless without it. Catherine said to stop saying that because he hears the other thing about being dumb.

Understanding the family's approach to Rodney's compliance to the medication for ADHD requires a more nuanced perspective than just them following the directions of the school. Both Catherine and Tanisha view Rodney's behavior as dulled while on the medication, so they do not necessarily follow the school's directions about taking it after school and on weekends. Furthermore, Catherine mentions how Rodney interpreted the teacher's comment about medication to mean he is "dumb," leading her to think they are being too harsh and not realizing how serious the side effects of the medication are ("he does not want to eat" and "he's not Rodney"). At the same time, she makes sure he is on medication during the school day, to the point of going to school to give him a pill before the teacher calls about it. There is another reason for such close monitoring of his medication; Catherine fears additional child welfare involvement if Tanisha's baby takes it by mistake, given they are staying in the house and the baby crawls all over the place. The coercive nature of the maze ultimately is not effective here as Catherine does not fully accept the institutional mandate about the medication, giving it to Rodney only part of the time.

Meanwhile, Catherine has to deal with a different institution regarding Edward's ADHD: the court. Edward was arrested the previous year for the third time in two years; this time, he allegedly stole a girl's headphones while on a public bus. She states in her first interview that Edward's troubles with the justice system started shortly after his father was released from prison four and a half years ago; his father went to prison when Edward was just a baby. Initially, getting involved in the court system helped Edward, as it led to his ADHD diagnosis; however multihousehold issues compromised the treatment, as Edward's father, with whom Edward was staying at the time, did not believe in ADHD medication and took him off of it. Catherine attributes Edward's ongoing court troubles to him not being on medication; he eventually gets placed in a group home for two months due to a probation violation, where he does start taking the medication. But when Edward is about to be released from a group home back to her household, Catherine describes the challenges in keeping him on medication. When Catherine asked the group home staff how to get the medication, they told her to take him to the emergency room right away. She instead made an appointment at a clinic for the following week because she didn't have time that day to go to the emergency room. However, the clinic required additional blood work before giving the medication. Four months later, the issue still isn't resolved even though Catherine has been trying to get the blood work. This delay means that Edward has not been on medication since he left the group home. Consider this phone conversation between Catherine and Edward's probation officer that I overheard while visiting Catherine:

> *Catherine:* I went today for the blood work because we needed the blood work for his—for the psychiatrist. But unfortunately, the computer was down. So, she told me when I come back on Wednesday with the other child [Rodney], she will have it ready for me so I can take it where they can get him on the med[ication] because they can't give him the medicine without the blood work.
>
> *Probation officer (on speakerphone):* I know, I explained to him (Edward) that he really needs his meds.
>
> *Catherine:* I know—I went down there today, that is what took me so long— after the ER—the clinic is right across the street.

The probation officer tells Edward simply that he "needs his meds" but ignores the institutional obstacles with the mental health clinic that Catherine is raising in the conversation. She does not offer any help to Catherine to expedite the matter, leaving it to her to keep going to the clinic to get this blood work. This poses several difficulties for Catherine, as she has arthritic knees, making it hard to walk and get around on public transportation, especially on the icy winter streets in January when this conversation occurred. She also is managing Rodney's health issues; in addition to ADHD, he has asthma, which is being triggered by the cold weather. Meanwhile Edward has started to act out and create trouble for Catherine in the home, endangering his probation status. A few weeks later, he is arrested after breaking curfew and interfering with an arrest of another person by a police officer. Catherine ultimately decides it might be better to keep him locked up—in part due to the mental health medication issues—versus having him come home. Later in the interview, she says: "I can't force him to take the medicine. What do you want me to do, then you're gonna call ACS if I knock him upside his mouth and put it in his mouth, then I go to jail. It's like you're damned if you do and you're damned if you don't. So, I'm thinking if they do it there [in the detention facility], this way he'll be on it." Beyond the issues in getting the medications in the first place, Catherine feels powerless in helping Edward if he does not want to take the medication on his own. Catherine specifically raises the threat of an ACS case and potential jail time as constraining her attempts now that he's outside of the group home. She turns to another institution for Edward (i.e., juvenile court) to help her because otherwise she is "damned if you do and you're damned if you don't."

It doesn't help that Edward's court case continually faces postponement (four times between February 21 and March 21) due to the delay in getting a mental health evaluation; while it seems only to be a month delay, the original evaluation was ordered nine months before but was never completed. At this point, it has been almost three months since Edward has been staying in detention waiting for the evaluation (he was arrested on January 31) and eight months since he was last on medication for his ADHD. After the last court date on March 21, where the evaluation was still not completed, Edward asked to go to placement for twelve months when he appeared in court for sentencing five days later (March 26). Catherine did not go to that last court date because she got called in to work. Here are my notes from a home visit right after this happened:

> She said it was his decision although she suspects his dad was the one who told him to do it. She thinks the dad told him that if he just did his time, he could get out without being on probation or anything. I asked how the defense lawyer reacted to that; she said it was Edward's choice. . . . She also mentions that the prosecutor said Catherine wanted 18 months, not 12. . . . When I talk about where Edward might get placed, Catherine refers to it as upstate a couple times. Edward is hoping to be placed closer to them. I ask if he will get passes; she says she hopes so before he goes away.

As Catherine is not in court during this discussion, the district attorney uses her words to underline the request for eighteen months, as opposed to Edward's idea of twelve months. While she did ask for eighteen months, it is not clear if Edward's lawyer could have talked with her beforehand about the advantages of pushing for twelve months instead. Edward is moved three weeks later to a new group home, which is a special education facility for developmentally disabled youth.[3]

While multiple agencies worked to address Edward and Rodney's ADHD, it was not a seamless or effective process for either child. Edward never got his medication and ultimately got arrested for probation violations, while Rodney interpreted the teacher's words about his medication as evidence that he was "dumb." Moreover, Catherine's experiences with her grandsons' mental health issues highlight the racialized character of those responses. Catherine faced the added stress of a new possible child welfare case, not only for Rodney, but for Tanisha's baby. Catherine also had to run around between the hospital, the mental health agency, and the court, which put her health at risk, given the wintertime conditions. Finally, the court appeared to compromise the mental health treatment for Edward, in that it faced extreme delays in getting him assessed for medication—penalizing him for the probation violations he accumulated as they awaited that mental health evaluation.[4]

For other families, finding treatment for a member's mental illness was compromised potentially by pursuing treatment for other co-occurring physical conditions. Josefina Delgado, a forty-nine-year-old Dominican mother, talks in an interview with my research assistant, Jerry, about Nhazul, her fifteen-year-old son, whose anxiety affects his eating habits, leading to potential obesity:

> *Josefina:* Sometimes he has a lot of anxiety and wants to eat everything.
>
> *Jerry:* You mentioned he has anxiety. When did his anxiety start?
>
> *Josefina:* He's always had it, but there are days when he eats more than others.

According to Josefina, Nhazul's mental health is directly related to his physical health. However, Josefina goes on to describe how the doctor discussed Nhazul's anxiety with them:

> *Jerry:* Have you told the doctor that maybe that's why he is overweight?
>
> *Josefina:* Uh-huh [yes].
>
> *Jerry:* What does the doctor say about his anxiety?
>
> *Josefina:* He talks to him. He tells him he has to control it.
>
> *Jerry:* How?
>
> *Josefina:* He says, "Nhazul, it's for your health. You have to understand that there is currently a lot of diabetes, high cholesterol, and high blood

pressure." You know, so, it runs in the family, because his grandmother has high cholesterol, has diabetes, has high blood pressure. And it runs in the family.

It is not clear from Josefina's answer if Nhazul is getting treated for anxiety. Her recollection of the doctor's response focuses on the physical conditions only. If in fact his anxiety is causing the weight gain, this interaction with the doctor is a missed opportunity to treat Nhazul effectively for both. Moreover, it appears that Josefina views the medical doctor's response as sufficient, not questioning how he addressed Nhazul's anxiety in the context of his obesity which he has to "control."

Poor families are faced with limited options to access mental health treatment. Many resort to calling the police, where it is not clear what will happen to the family and its journey in the multi-institutional maze. As discussed in chapter 3, Talia Thomas called the police when her son, Samuel, hit her, with the ultimate goal of having the court mandate mental health treatment. That led to delayed treatment as well as more institutional involvements (i.e., child welfare and a delinquency case in court).[5] In contrast, Carmelo Strong, a fifteen-year-old Latino, has asthma and ADHD; he also reported having suicidal thoughts after his mom's death several years ago. His fifty-seven-year-old grandmother, Iris, gives him pills for ADHD; if she forgets, she goes to his school to give it to him. One year ago, they had to call the police because Carmelo was "acting crazy," according to Iris. Her daughter (Carmelo's aunt, Carmin) said he was "throwing papers, throwing water at us." Iris and her daughter describe the situation in more detail in an interview:

Iris: No, the police came because he was acting crazy, he also wanted to cut himself.

Carmin: It's just that every time we call the ambulance, they send the police, because of his behavior. . . . Yes, because the first time it happened, when he was throwing paper and water, we called an ambulance, and the police came and took him. They let him go. They didn't leave him there [in the hospital]. He was evaluated and they let him go two days later or the following day. So, a week later, they called that they were going to send a social worker to evaluate his behavior. . . . When she came to interview him that afternoon, he was ignoring her, and he was throwing things. . . . She had to call the ambulance that day.

Leslie: And after she called, the police came with the ambulance?

Iris: Yes, they tied him up. They had to tie him up.

Leslie: What did the doctor say? Was there a therapist? A psychiatrist?

Iris: Yes, he was evaluated.

Leslie: And what was it?

Iris: I don't know, but they told me to call them if I needed anything.

Carmin: They changed the medication.

The family still is not clear as to his mental health condition or treatment, except for needing new medication. What is analytically important here is to see that the police now have become the first responders in this situation—which in this case, seems to work well with the psychiatric social worker and hospital to which he was admitted.

The Medina family's experience dealing with their youth's mental health shows both the opportunities and disadvantages found in the multi-institutional maze. Fifteen-year-old Carlos Medina got diagnosed with bipolar depression after his thirty-nine-year-old mother, Maria, called the police on him for breaking a window in their home during a fight with his twenty-one-year-old brother. She mentioned in our interview that he had been giving her trouble at home, disrespecting her, cursing her out, not doing any chores and doing whatever he wants. The police took him to a hospital for evaluation versus detention. She says his recent diagnosis now makes sense, given his behavior: "I knew it because of his temper. Five minutes he loves you and five minutes he hates you." While that incident led to a psychiatric (versus a justice) intervention, he might face a different response the next time he has an incident that could be related to his depression, especially if the family does not specify that it is a mental health issue or if the police who respond do not have sufficient mental health training.[6] And yet at the same time, Maria and Carlos deal with the challenge of managing a person's treatment across households. As discussed in the last chapter, this multihousehold situation does provide an opportunity for Maria to focus on her other involvements; however, she also acknowledges in her interview that it poses difficulties for his mental health condition. That is, it is hard to manage his medication because he goes over to his father's house where she does not know what happens:

Maria: The thing is when he go [there] I get him some medication. I don't know if he drink it and I dunno if he throw them away. But he come with the empty bottle and I dunno like I said if he drink it or throw it [away].

Leslie: And you don't know if you can trust his father's family to [give it?]

Maria: Right.

While he has now a diagnosis and medication to help address his volatile moods, the multihousehold family makes it difficult to monitor Carlos's illness. The implications of Carlos not taking the medication go beyond his behavior within the family; he also now has a court case for vandalizing school property, which monitors his actions even more. So if he starts acting out due to not taking his medication, it could potentially lead to probation violations.

In sum, mental health conditions expose the ways that institutional mismatch can manifest across temporal, multihousehold, and concurrent institutional involvements and, in turn, propel poor minority families deeper into the multi-institutional maze.[7] That is, poor and minority families have few options for treatment for a mentally ill family member, often relying upon institutions (e.g., police, schools, hospital emergency rooms) that end up penalizing them versus helping them. The unpredictability of families' journeys in the maze stems from not knowing which agency will respond at what time and in which ways to the family member's mental illness. Trying to access treatment via these various agencies also does not accommodate the influence of past involvements shaping family understandings of treatment or address how multiple households affect families' ability to manage the treatment.

Domestic Abuse

While families did not discuss domestic abuse with me as frequently as mental health issues, some did mention it in the context of other institutional involvements. Their experiences reveal how the institutional interventions were insufficient or incompatible with the needs that resulted from the abuse. This section first addresses how the temporal aspect to multi-institutional involvement could further compound the trauma related to child abuse and then turns to how concurrent or multihousehold involvements also lead to incomplete institutional responses to domestic abuse.

Catherine's family does not receive effective institutional interventions regarding child abuse, which in this instance, also affects Edward's ongoing delinquency court case. During an interview, Catherine tells me that she filed an order of protection for Edward against his dad. His dad was in prison for ten years due to the drug bust that was discussed earlier in the chapter. Since his release, he has been trying to rebuild his relationship with his two sons, Edward and Shawn. However, that process has not been going well. The father had an open child welfare case after the school reported seeing welt marks on Edward's brother, Shawn; he apparently beat Shawn with an extension cord as a form of discipline. She explains in an interview why she got the order of protection for Edward:

> I had to get one for Edward because . . . Edward's father had still been coming [around]. When he sees something on Facebook, he comes here and he punch him all up in his face and beat him up. One day I was looking out the window, and I saw his father punch him. So, I ran downstairs. I opened the car door. . . . He [Edward's father] cussed me out, "That's my son." I just pushed Edward in the door and locked it. . . . And then one day . . . he [Edward's dad] said, "Ma, I got your money the person owe. Send Edward downstairs to get it." So, I said, "Okay." I sent Edward down there. Rodney's screaming, "Nanna, he's hitting him." He came upstairs holding his face. He posted something on Facebook like he was getting high and he got some girl up in here, which was a lie, trying to make himself look good. . . . His father punched him in his face for that. And they said I could lose all the kids because I'm not—failure to protect Edward. So, if I'm not protecting him, that means I'm not gonna protect no one in here. So, I had to go through that, which his father's pissed off about that.

Edward asked her to file this order of protection against his father.[8] But Catherine also did so because she was afraid of more institutional involvement, namely, for her other children in the household. That increased the level of conflict between her and her son, Edward's father. Yet while she still wants to work with the agencies to find a way to reconcile with Edward's father, the institutions apparently are not able to do so. She states that the child welfare and probation staff refuse to work with the dad. Later in the interview, she explains how she discussed her view of child welfare (ACS) with Shawn's social worker from a court agency related to his PINS case:

> "I'm tired of ACS," I said, "because they come in. You tell 'em the things you need help with and all of this; they don't do anything." I said, "They got the meeting for my son to come in, which the ACS lady was like, 'Whoa.'" My son's very aggressive . . . their [Edward and Shawn's] lawyer won't even talk to my son. She don't like the way he talks to her. . . . The probation lady said, "I don't want Edward around him; he's too aggressive for the way he speaks. He thinks he knows everything and wants to be right." So, nobody want to work with my son. 'Cause I figured maybe we'd go to counseling, all of us together. So, it wasn't working.

When I asked Sarah, the director of the intensive mentoring program working with Edward, during our interview about Catherine's comments, she didn't answer directly, speaking generally about the organizational conflicts between child welfare and the delinquency court: "I wasn't understanding why one child [Shawn] had an order of protection and the other child [Edward] didn't, but it was made clear it was the same exact offense on the child, but they [child welfare] allowed Edward to decide that he wanted to stay in contact with this man [Edward and Shawn's father]. . . . Once they learn a child they are involved with has a probation case, their immediate response is, 'Why aren't you remanding him?' We've been told that numerous times."

Sarah provided some insight into the lack of coordination between child welfare and delinquency court—the former simply turns the case over to the latter, specifically asking probation to focus on controlling the youth's "wild" behavior. The issue for child welfare is no longer the parental abuse but the youth's "delinquent" actions; the institution then is individualizing and shifting blame onto the youth. When Edward was staying in a group home the year before, the staff let the dad see him, even though Catherine told them not to do so, because of the beatings mentioned above. According to Sarah, the group home staff told her and the court that Catherine never told them about this physical abuse by Edward's father. Regardless of how that communication lapse occurred, it created more conflict between Edward, Catherine, and Edward's dad: Edward asked Catherine to help keep his father away but when she did, he still saw his dad, which increased the animosity between Catherine and her son, as well as between Catherine and Edward. While it is unclear how or why the child welfare agency allowed this situation to escalate, it ultimately led to Edward opting to ask for more permanent placement in a long-term secure residential facility, which the mentoring staff attributes to him wanting to get away from all this family turmoil. Sarah explains: "He [Edward] is not our first child who's requested to be placed. . . . Based on Edward's familial history, I'm not surprised that he felt more secure being placed than returning to his home. And like I said, we had another child in a similar situation. So, whenever kids are requesting placement . . . it's just an indication to me that it's a safety issue, a safety concern on his part." Note that Sarah refers to Edward's "familial history" as the motivation behind his request for placement and not the institutional conflicts between the juvenile court and child welfare (which she raised earlier in the interview). So the outcome is framed solely as a result of the family's situation and, more specifically, the youth's choice. How this placement will affect Edward's navigation of the maze moving forward is undetermined. Yet what is clear is that the lingering effects of the physical abuse he experienced from his father remain untreated.

At the same time, there are other issues going on in and outside of the household that now shape how Catherine views Edward's court case. While Edward was in detention awaiting the mental health evaluation, Catherine shared with me during a home visit some new information she learned from Rodney:

> Catherine said that Rodney is going through some stuff and that she needs to focus on him. He told her some disturbing news a couple days ago: Edward touched him inappropriately and said he could do it whenever he wanted. Rodney told Shawn, who started a huge fight with Edward; Catherine at the time didn't know what it was about. Rodney didn't want Catherine to get mad at him or Edward. . . . Apparently, his other cousin, Carrie (Tanisha's daughter), also molested him. That incident came out in group therapy with ACS when Rodney mentioned it and that was the first time Catherine knew about that. Carrie is no longer allowed to stay in her home now. . . . She is asking for Edward to go away for 18 months in maximum security. She then says that is what he wants and is asking for. I'm not sure what that means. She says both she and Edward were crying in court but it's time for tough love. . . . She says that she can't have him back in the house—especially after what happened with Rodney.

Her reasoning in asking the court to place Edward for eighteen months is informed by this new information that Rodney told her.[9] I asked Catherine for an update about Rodney's counseling for the alleged sexual abuse:

> Catherine says that Rodney has started going to see a counselor; he asked the counselor where Dr. M. was (for his ADHD meds). The counselor said she was just there to help him talk about some of his problems. He asked which problems; his brother (Edward) is in jail or a few other serious issues about his family. Catherine laughs as she says she told the counselor that he thinks he is an old man. She laughs some more as she says he just told her all of our business.

This anecdote encapsulates many facets to the multi-institutional maze. Rodney already sees someone for ADHD, so he initially is confused about the reason to see this counselor. When the counselor explains she wants to talk about his problems, he does not see those as separate from the many "serious issues about his family." Finally, Catherine's joke about a five-year-old thinking "he is an old man" reveals a more serious question related to family multi-institutional involvement: What is the impact on a young child who has experienced so much institutional intervention in his own life as well as those of his family's "business"? A few months after this excerpt, Catherine tells me that Rodney stopped going to counseling for the alleged abuse by Edward. This does not mean he has "recovered" from the alleged trauma per se; Catherine explains what happened during a home visit:

> I ask if Rodney is still in counseling. Catherine says no because he didn't want it. The counselor called and Rodney was saying something like, "If she is not Dr. M (who he sees monthly for meds), then I don't need to see her. I already go to a school counselor." The counselor said not to force him to come if he didn't want to. Catherine said she tried to get him to go but he refused. She said okay. I ask if this counseling was because of what he said Edward did. She said yes. She then said that Edward and he sat down together to talk about it—Edward of course denied it. Shawn said he remembers Rodney telling him what Edward did but he didn't see it. I ask Catherine what she believes happened. She says that she believes Rodney but then again, usually if that happens, the person doesn't want to be around the abuser. She says maybe Rodney is okay with that because he is so young. But I can hear the doubt in her voice about his story.

The counselor didn't help Catherine or Rodney here, providing no clear resolution about the alleged abuse and leaving Catherine with an underlying doubt about who to believe and how to address the situation. While in some ways the counselor is respecting Rodney's wishes to not continue, Catherine is conflicted about how to deal with both Edward and Rodney. It is perhaps easier now that Edward is in a long-term court placement. But it also is important to note that Catherine is trying to work with institutions for both Rodney and Edward's mental health and domestic abuse issues; in this instance, it is the counselor's advice to let Rodney dictate the treatment that leads her to stop.

Catherine's family is not the only one to discuss the failures of the system to deal with its issues of abuse, adding a new light to the temporal element of multi-institutional involvement. As discussed in chapter 2, Ethel Evans had to deal with a child welfare system that disrupted her living situation with her two nieces and two nephews for months, making them move from their apartment into a bug-infested apartment in another borough. Yet Ethel also insists the system did not help the children deal with the traumatic issues associated with the abuse they experienced by their mother and her boyfriend. Their mother was arrested for rape of a minor, and her boyfriend was arrested for molesting one of his girlfriend's daughters. In this interview excerpt, Ethel goes into more detail about the institutional mismatch in how the juvenile

court is responding now to Micah's current delinquency case, given this
past child abuse:

> I think that the system didn't help these kids. And I feel the system still is
> not helping these kids. I don't. . . . What is the court doing? . . . They either
> arrest him, put them in a group home and then or put them into . . . detention
> homes. . . . The point is they don't help them because the only thing that it
> does is make them even more angrier. And then they do what has happened
> with my nephew—they put them on probation and he's back home. Noth-
> ing's changed. . . . He does all the right things just to come back home to go
> back into the same old routine where he shut down.

Ethel groups the child welfare agency's response and delinquency
court as "the system," which technically is correct. In New York City,
Family Court handles both child welfare and delinquency matters.
However, these cases are not concurrent, so the judge can only focus on
her nephew's delinquency case for being defiant in school, truant, and
having marijuana right outside school. That proves limiting and frustrating to Ethel, who says the child welfare system "didn't help" before
and the court is "still not helping" now. Instead, it is making Micah
"angrier," after which the court further penalizes him for acting out,
versus treating his issues to help him not "shut down" while at home.

Shifting attention to the parents who are victims of abuse, several
mothers talked about experiencing domestic violence from their former
or current partners. For some, the insufficient response of one institution unintentionally can spark new institutional involvements. Michelle
Wilson talks about the latest incident with the father of her son, Kevin,
who has been abusive towards her before.[10] Michelle says Kevin's father
always had a work ethic, but he just drank and got violent on her. After
this latest incident, she obtained a five-year order of protection and he
spent two months in jail:

> Michelle talks more about the incident where Kevin's dad tried to kick
> the door down. It was Father's Day and he showed up too drunk to see
> Kevin. . . . She was going to let him see Kevin when she smelled the alcohol
> on his breath. So, she started to close the door when he stuck his foot in the
> frame and then opened the door. He came into the living room and started to
> choke Michelle in front of the kids. . . . She managed to push him out of the
> apartment and lock the door; he then proceeded to kick the door at least 15
> times and the door was on the hinges. . . . He was in jail for two months; the
> district attorney called her before he got out. He hasn't come by since—even
> though they did walk by each other [on the street]. . . . He saw her and she
> saw him; they didn't speak as they passed by each other. She says he finally
> has learned that if he does come by, he'll go to jail.

In this instance, it does appear that the justice system is protecting Michelle from her son's father, who ends up spending time in jail; however, there are limits, as he does get out after only two months, and the order of protection doesn't prevent them from bumping into each other in the neighborhood. The point here is that this incident leads to an additional investigation by child welfare (ACS), not on the father, but on Michelle, who has custody of the children:

> A couple days after the last incident . . . Michelle was cleaning up the house around midnight when the doorbell rang. It was ACS looking to do an emergency inspection and they want to make sure the dad doesn't have any parental rights. . . . They didn't remove Kevin, but the case is open for two months. Michelle didn't sound upset by it; she said she has nothing to hide and the case is unfounded. She imagined it would be different if she smoked drugs or something. I asked why the caseworker came so late; she says she doesn't know but the DA [district attorney] could have called it in so they had to come immediately without any notice. Now they call in advance and she expects they'll close the case in two months.

The irony here is that she and her children were victims and yet she has another institutional intervention added to her journey in the maze. While Michelle is unconcerned about the child welfare visits, as she "has nothing to hide," she is still at the mercy of their assessment of her parenting as acceptable. What also is missing here is any mention of counseling for Michelle or her children to deal with the fact that the father physically attacked her in front of them. From what Michelle says here, the child welfare agency—like probation in Micah and Edward's court cases—is focusing on just one specific issue of the physical safety of the children, versus a more holistic view that also includes the financial aspects of child support (which Michelle tells me during another visit that the dad is not paying) and the psychological issues associated with witnessing such violence between the parents.

As these examples reveal, domestic abuse can highlight the institutional mismatch in agencies' partial responses; those piecemeal solutions often lead to increased institutional involvements for the families, which still do not address the abuse but end up blaming the victims in various ways. Poor and minority families often experience that limited and potentially more punitive institutional response. That is, Ethel talked about the ongoing and untreated trauma for her nieces and nephews after years of abuse, which is now playing out in her nephew Micah's delinquency court case. In both Micah and Edward's delinquency cases, the court staff are not addressing those abuse issues but rather are focusing on teaching the teenagers how to take responsibility for their actions. Catherine's account of Edward and his father suggests that even the institutions mandated to address the abuse are limited in their response; while child welfare and probation officers saw the father's aggression and refused to work with him, they still did not stop him from visiting Edward while he was in a group home.[11] Michelle's situation also shows how the victim of domestic abuse gets further victimized as she has to now deal with an open child welfare case after her son's father physically attacked them.

IMMIGRATION

Immigrant families face unique sets of challenges in navigating the multi-institutional maze as they have two cultural frames of reference and two sets of systems in their home country and the United States to consider.[12] These differences further expose the unpredictability of families' journeys in the maze and instances of institutional mismatch.

The Cabrera Family

Diego Cabrera is forty-eight years old and works full-time as a manager of a carwash; his wife, Sofia, is forty-four years old and is a homemaker. She has short, dark brown hair that is cut fairly simply, and she wears no or minimal makeup. She dresses in loose clothing and has a softer physique and demeanor compared to Diego, who is very physically fit, with salt and pepper hair and a tan complexion like he has been in the sun a lot. They immigrated from Uruguay over twenty years ago; originally, they were in Massachusetts for two years before moving to New York City. They live with their two younger sons, sixteen-year-old Richard and nineteen-year-old Mark, in a one-bedroom apartment that they converted into a two-bedroom by putting up a wall to split the bedroom into two. Sofia also watches her eighteen-month-old granddaughter, Kayla, who is the daughter of their twenty-one-year-old son, Henry; she stays over several days during the week while Henry and his wife are working.

Their apartment is on a residential street just off a main thoroughfare in a multiethnic neighborhood in Queens, New York. Their street has a combination of large apartment buildings like theirs and smaller individual houses. Their street also has several different places of worship—Buddhist center (it looks like a house), Jehovah's Witness (English and

Korean signs), as well as another denomination across the street. Their apartment is a corner unit; it is dark due to the shades being drawn. It is very clean and tidy. The living/dining room is fairly large, with a marble-like dining room table with a plastic covering on top. They also have a small beagle-mix–like dog which has its own futon-style bed in the room.

Over the last five years, the Cabreras's three sons have gone through juvenile court for delinquency offenses (assault, vandalism, trespassing/robbery). Henry was arrested after violating an order of protection and beating up someone who had to stay in the hospital for three days. Mark set a garbage can on fire in the park with a friend and paid a fine. Richard is currently still going through the court process after being arrested for trespassing and robbery. Sofia stopped working as a housekeeper once Henry got arrested to focus on their children. Like other immigrant families, the Cabreras have difficulties communicating with the court staff. While Diego speaks English fluently, he cannot attend most court hearings due to his work schedule. Sofia, who does go to the hearings, understands but does not feel comfortable talking in English. So while other parents who do speak English also don't often speak up in the court hearings, it is harder for Sofia, as she can't express herself even with an interpreter present.[13]

Cultural Differences between Parents and Children

One typical challenge for immigrant families arises when the "children learn English and adopt American ways far faster than do their immigrant parents" (Waters et al. 2010: 1169).[14] This could lead to institutional involvement in two scenarios. First, the conflicts arising from the family's different views of their own internal dynamics become known to others outside the household.[15] Second, the parents' expectations of institutions in the United States are shaped by their experiences as children in their home country. The Cabreras's experience with their sons' court cases reflects the first scenario. Below, Diego discusses how he sees Richard's case now that it is near to being closed:

> Diego said Richard is doing much better, talking more and getting along better with Michael and Henry. He added later that he never would talk back to his parents or say he will do it later because you didn't have that choice in Uruguay. He says that caused some conflict with his sons because he didn't understand how this generation is different. But now he does.

He goes into more detail about this conflict in an interview eight months later, after Richard opts to go to a group home for several months in lieu of probation:

> *Diego:* He [Richard] told me that "I know I was upset about what happened with you, but I understand now. I understand what you did, it's just the best for me." That's the only thing you want him to understand. Everything we do for you is for your best. I don't want you to like just be every day on the street, not doing anything and just gonna end up on the system all the time.
>
> *Leslie:* I don't mean to go back in the past, but are you referring to—was he referring to when you called the police on him?
>
> *Diego:* Yeah, he was kind of upset a little bit.
>
> *Leslie:* Yeah, sure.
>
> *Diego:* I understand because he said probably, "My father, he shouldn't be doing that because I don't know. He said he loves me but that's not the way he shows me the way he loves me." But I told him I was, "Listen, it was a situation that I have to do what I have to do. So you gotta understand me, as a father; one day you're gonna be a father and you don't want to see your kid going through these things because it's annoying. It's frustrating." So I say whatever happens, it happens but now it's just looking forward, just focusing on what you want to accomplish.

Diego would call the police on his son, Richard, if he was out late, leading to curfew violations which generated further court involvement. Diego's actions strained their relationship as Richard got mad at his father as well. This conflict also happened with US-born parents who talked about differences between their generation and their children who don't listen to them. At the same time, it does show how immigrant families might get caught up in institutional systems in ways that US-born families may know to avoid, whether by class privilege (e.g., getting therapy versus calling the police to deal with a teenager's problematic behavior) or race (e.g., not involving the police if they are distrustful of the system).

Those from the 1.5 generation invoke similar issues of what it is like for them "back home" compared to here. Michelle Wilson came to the United States when she was seven years old, yet she refers to her childhood experiences back in Jamaica when she talks about her expectations of her children and institutions. For example, she recently pulled her two-year-old son from his current day care because she did not think it was strict enough, as compared to her school experiences in Jamaica:

We started talking about Kevin and day care. . . . She wants more structure for Kevin. . . . She has in mind a Head Start program nearby. I ask if he is too young for that program and she said no, he just has to be two years and nine months, which he probably will be by the time he gets off the waiting list. . . . She said she went to school at a young age as well in Jamaica, but it was much stricter than it is here. There, you had to pay for lunch, walk to and from school and the teachers were not as nice.

Like Diego, Michelle seeks a more authoritarian type of program for her son to replicate the dynamics that she had as a child back home. While this instance does not seem problematic, as Kevin is only a toddler, the implications for her navigating the maze are twofold: (1) she has to find a program for Kevin which takes time and paperwork, adding more turns in the maze; and (2) it hinders her resources in navigating or exiting the maze, as she cannot look for full-time work while Kevin is no longer in day care and staying at home.

Navigating Two Systems across Borders

For immigrant families who have to negotiate two systems in different countries at the same time, several other challenges can arise. A family's multi-institutional involvement can get complicated if the families have to go back and forth or if the organizations' demands require documentation across borders. Regarding the former, consider this fieldnote excerpt from Sofia and Diego Cabrera when I ask how they keep in contact with Diego's parents in Uruguay:

Diego mentions speaking to his mom over the phone, so I ask if he and Sofia have gone back to visit. He says no. I ask if his family comes over here; he said his parents came to visit three times over the years. Now they don't because they are too old. Last time, his dad had a medical problem, so he brought all his medicine with him. He ran out and they had a hard time getting more because the medication is different here and he needs to see a doctor. They were supposed to come for six months but after three, the mom wanted to go back. Diego said they had a six-month visa, so he convinced them to stay until the end of the visa.

While those of us who travel internationally might relate to the uncomfortable situation of having to get medication while abroad but not knowing the generic name to access it, this excerpt also shows how families' cultural capital as knowledgeable patients can be compromised in that instance. The Cabreras could not transfer their understanding regarding the necessary medication and treatment for Diego's father from their home country to the United States. The implications for the family are that they remain physically apart. The Cabreras have lived in the United States for over twenty years, and the grandparents have only come three times. While this might be simply due to age and money to travel, it is also informed by the grandfather's experience with the health care system here.

Claudia Desoto, a fifty-two-year-old Latina, reveals an additional complexity in how an institution in one country can prevent her access to a different institution in another country. She discusses in an interview how she wanted to send her fifteen-year-old son, Miguel, to Colombia over the summer so that he can get braces. Because he has an open delinquency case in New York City Family Court for trespassing, she first wants to confirm with his lawyer that he can go. However, she cannot get a clear answer in a timely manner, as she describes in an interview:

> I think she did her job well. . . . She has many cases. . . . The only thing was that sometimes we would call and she would not respond. . . . You know, he is in probation and I had a problem with him trying to get his braces done because the insurance did not want to cover it. . . . So I wanted to take advantage of some vacations and send him to his father in Colombia and have them done there. . . . We got tired of calling and calling her. . . . She never responds. . . . Then I ask myself, what if I had an emergency and I had to leave the country with him? How would I be able to petition for that? . . . That is also why he [Miguel] says he does not like her because she never responds to us. . . . When she got back to me, the vacation time had passed and he had started classes again. . . . I explained to her the reason why . . . and she said you would have to call me like two months prior, so we tried again, and she still did not respond back to us. . . . Since then I have not been in contact with her.

Claudia has resources in one country but cannot use them, as she is being constrained by institutions (e.g., the juvenile court) in another. That is, she is trying to follow the appropriate procedures in the juvenile court, seeking permission through her son's lawyer for him to leave the country without endangering his probation status. Yet the lawyer is unresponsive even after the mom tries again to work within her suggested timeframe (two months). The results are that both the mom and son lost trust in the lawyer, which does not help Miguel's court case, and they can't use the resources they do have in Colombia.

Finally, the experience of Gabriela Garcia, a twenty-four-year-old Mexican mother, in trying to get health insurance exemplifies the ways that immigration further complicates the documentation issues in institutional involvements. She lives with her husband, their five children, and her father-in-law in a one-bedroom apartment in the Bronx. She hurt her foot last year while working as a housecleaner and now needs surgery. However, she is caught in the following bind in how to improve her health to get back to work: she has high blood pressure that needs to be lower before she can get the surgery. She can't get surgery without health insurance and yet she can't work until she has surgery. Meanwhile she has already been to the emergency room three times due to the high blood pressure. Here is how she explains her dilemma in an interview:

> They [at Weingart hospital] weren't able to help me, because they asked for a lot of requirement. They asked when my grandmother was born. They needed my grandmother's birth certificate, my great-grandmother's and my mother's. And so, it's not possible for me to have all that information, because my mother is in Mexico. I didn't even meet my great-grandmother. . . . I told my social worker [at another clinic where her daughter goes] about that and she couldn't believe it: "Why are they asking for so much information?" And I told her, "This isn't the first time I try to get checked at a hospital and I had never been asked for all that information." Since I had been seen at that hospital for my daughter, after she was born, they didn't want to check me anymore. They said no, because I didn't have medical insurance and that if I went—I just went to the appointment you get after birth, and after that, they were no longer able to see me.

Gabriela's experience highlights the combined temporal and geographical challenges in institutional involvement that is further compounded by immigration. According to Gabriela, the staff at Weingart demands four generations of birth certificates to sign her up for insurance. Getting those documents would be hard enough to do in the United States but infinitely more difficult if one had to go to another country to retrieve them.[16] While it is not perhaps the official policy or perhaps even what the caseworker meant, it is what she understood. Even though her social worker doubts Weingart's account, she also does not appear able to help rectify the insurance issue, as Gabriela can't get treated there. The irony here is that Gabriela has this social worker because when her daughter was born at Weingart, the doctor pulled so hard that the baby's shoulder was dislocated, and her arm was fractured. So, Weingart sent Gabriela and her baby to a clinic for therapy where the social worker started helping Gabriela. In contrast to middle-class or rich families who have insurance through their employment or even could potentially pay up front for this medical care, Gabriela is caught in between these systems with the ultimate result of not having insurance and thus, not being able to escape the bind of poor health–no work to help support her family.

In short, immigration highlights the unpredictability in families' journeys in the multi-institutional maze. For some poor immigrant families, unexpected forms of institutional involvement could result from parental expectations based on traditions from their home country, such as Diego calling the police on his youngest son, Richard, whose behavior seemed unacceptable to Diego. That cultural conflict led to a protracted juvenile court case that lasted over a year. Similarly, Michelle's taking her son out of day care seems like a typical parental response; however, her standards are informed by her experiences in Jamaica, which may or may not be met in another program in the United States. The time and resources she spends to find a new program take away from her efforts to focus on other institutional involvements such as Shakera's behavioral issues and her own health issues, as well as more job opportunities. Immigrant families also experience unique forms of institutional mismatch when dealing with two different systems for the same issue in two different countries. Diego's family remains separated, due to different medical systems not being able to accommodate their sick members (i.e., Diego's father). Finally, the paperwork requirements for institutions assume that one has the official documents to establish eligibility, which for many poor immigrants such as Gabriela, may not be a guarantee.

CONCLUSION

Navigating and getting out of the multi-institutional maze is already a daunting task given the concurrent, temporal, and multihousehold issues discussed in the previous chapters. The contingency factors of mental illness, domestic violence, and immigration only compound those challenges, both in how families and institutions act and respond. It can be disruptive for any family trying to find the right treatment and resources for the mentally ill family member, but it is especially so for poor minority families who have to seek those out from various public institutions. Families' experiences with domestic violence reveal the insufficiency of these institutions in providing services for those families to navigate the maze. That is, untreated or partially treated trauma due to childhood abuse affects how adults and children alike view and distrust other institutions as part of the same "system." Victims of domestic violence can get further traumatized in other systems such as child welfare that ends up punishing them for violence they experienced. These factors could be interrelated, such as when the trauma from past domestic violence affects one's mental health. Moreover, we often talk about the cycle of violence being replicated across generations without considering more thoroughly how the institutions themselves contribute to perpetuating that cycle. Immigrant families can get further caught in the maze as more turns and walls get added if conflicts between immigrant parents and children increase their institutional involvements.

These contingencies, compounded with the other factors in the maze, show how families' journey through the multi-institutional maze can be fraught with unexpected land mines that lurch the family forward, sideways, or backward in the maze. They also reveal the institutional mismatch in families' journeys in the maze. The institutional mismatch could come from instances where agencies do not have enough information to respond, or they have the information but no ability to respond. It also could stem from situations where different agencies provide only partial solutions, yet their combined efforts often do not add up to any meaningful resolution for the families. Those piecemeal responses foster an unpredictability as well to families' experiences, given that the same institution could respond differently to the same issue, providing services to help or to surveil families even more. The conclusion, though, would not be to suggest that institutions should stop helping these families; rather, we need to stop viewing families' outcomes only as a result of their supposed inability to meet institutional expectations. The contingencies explored here beg the question of how institutions can harness the right amount of information in the right timing so that the right agency can respond with the right resources. A related question would be how institutions respond in situations where those goals are unattainable. The next and final chapter attempts to address those two questions.

CHAPTER 6

Conclusion

*Reflections on the Maze
and Practical Steps Forward*

This book has shown the complexity of poor families' lives, particularly as they seek out and are compelled to engage in institutions to help or "correct" their situations. The families' journeys in the multi-institutional maze are not easy to navigate, and for many, seemingly impossible to complete. The way to understand families' journeys is not to assume that nothing can be done to alter them, but rather to consider the challenges created by the concurrent, temporal, multihousehold, and contingent elements to their institutional involvements.

We also must acknowledge two often overlooked or misunderstood facets to these families' experiences in dealing with multiple institutions. One is the amount of effort that they expend to deal with the numerous eligibility requirements and compliance issues. While the common stereotype is that poor families are "welfare dependent" or not willing to work, the reality is that they are constantly having to prove their worth to institutions in ways that often do not yield meaningful results to anyone. Families also demonstrate initiative and have to spend enormous amounts of energy to survive and maintain any kind of tenuous stability. It is more apt to depict their experiences as ducks in the water: while they appear to be gliding along the surface, they are frantically paddling underneath to navigate through the water. We need to recognize and acknowledge that effort—which, again, is often required by the institutions in attempts to establish their "deservedness" for services—instead of continually condemning them for doing "nothing." We also need to situate families' actions within the larger economic context, to evaluate whether the income and benefits associated with the jobs they might do are sufficient enough to replace the supports (e.g., health insurance) provided by the institutions in which they currently are involved. If they are not, it is only logical that parents opt to continue working part-time or not at all, as they are viewing the larger picture of how to provide for their children and themselves.

That leads to the second facet about the institutions themselves. We must recognize how institutions actually play a large role in perpetuating family poverty. I found that institutions were often at a loss to address the problems before them. In fact, the institutions featured in this book sometimes made those problems *worse* and more deeply entrenched as they attempted to find ways to respond to families. I am referring to the untreated trauma related to abuse, the institutional mismatch of services, and the cumulative effects of interventions over time, especially if they are only partial or incomplete responses.[1] We also often talk about these institutions as the collective unit of the "state," or that we can improve the services if we just find better ways to coordinate between them. Yet, as this book has shown, institutions are not so unified or clear-cut in how they work with families. The same institution can both help and hurt families, depending on the situation. So it is not easy or necessarily fruitful to continue discussing ways to better streamline or coordinate among these agencies.

Where does that leave us? If families get trapped in the maze, what would be a path forward? Put simply, we must change our approach. Unless we recognize these two facets of poor families' experiences with multiple institutions, we can never truly address how to effectively respond to their needs and help them move out of poverty. This last chapter considers some principles and possible options for future policy reform.

THREE GUIDING THOUGHTS TO REFORM

In some ways, it is impossible to envision a rational system based on situations that are unpredictable, as is the case for many of the families' experiences in the maze. Yet I don't mean to suggest we need to get rid of these institutions. At the same time, I do not think that simply allocating more money to the institutions is the solution either.[2] In short, public institutions and the services they provide are still needed—for the families and for the greater good of the society in general. The question is how to make institutions more responsive to families' issues. Below are some principles I believe need to be considered in any kind of meaningful reform.

New Definitions of Family

The definition of *family* in both policy reform and research needs to be expanded in two ways. First, we need to reconsider the emphasis on marriage as the goal for stabilizing families. While I am not questioning the research about the stressors of multi-partner fertility on families, the reality is that many poor parents are unmarried and their decisions to not marry stem largely from economic uncertainty.[3] To continue to insist upon marriage as the pathway to a family's self-reliance or social mobility is unrealistic unless we stabilize the economic uncertainty of those couples' situations. It also further perpetuates the current class inequalities in contemporary patterns in marriage formation.[4] Moreover, it is not just two parents that can support children. Extended family networks, including friends and community, can play a huge role in that regard. Consider how marriage "stabilizes" a household or not, based on a few of the families in my study: Eileen Fouskas was still married, even though she and her husband lived separately for over ten years and are not working together as a united front for their children's institutional involvements. In contrast, Talia and Michael Thomas were never legally married (which I found out months into doing fieldwork) but considered themselves as such. He was an active father and stepfather to all of her children. Meanwhile, Catherine Bryant's family was perhaps the most complicated to unpack regarding partners and households, yet it had one of the strongest bonds between them of all the families in the study. Perhaps the takeaway message is that we accept families' structures as they are and not hold them to the standard of marriage.

Second, we need to pay attention to the diversity in how family members deal with these institutions, with variations across generations and households. While Leisy Lopez did have to give up custody of her children, similar to her mother, she did not expose them to child or sexual abuse in the same way that her mother did. Her adult children also have had different pathways to social mobility so far: two of her sons are in college, her daughter is pursuing a GED, and two other sons have been in prison. In addition, while Tanisha does not appear to be working now, her mother, Catherine, is constantly pushing herself to work harder, as she does with Tanisha's daughter, Latisha, who is about to graduate from high school. In addition, while two of her sons did end up in prison for drug dealing with Edward's father also having several child abuse cases open against him, Catherine's younger son has a stable job as a delivery truck driver and is married with children. Those nuances need to be recognized to dispel the myth about "welfare-dependent families," as if all members have the same approach to institutions or face the same chances of getting out of poverty.

Better Management Is Not Necessarily the Answer

This book's findings point to the futility of insisting that better management within an institution or increased collaborations between institutions can address the complexities of families' problems.[5] As shown by Gigi Hernandez's attempts to access treatment for her diabetes, the partnership between two medical institutions can lead to more confusion between the staff in one of those institutions (the clinic and hospital) as to where she should go for what services. Similarly, Leisy's problems with renewing Kobe's SSI benefits stem not just from her failed efforts to get the paperwork in on time. She has a bevy of staff to help her (e.g., her supportive housing counselor, doctors, and psychiatrist), but none have the significant expertise across institutions to help her resolve the situation. In short, the institutions with which she interacts—hospital, supportive housing, mental health, disability, schools—are not set up to be flexible enough to deal with her multiple and interrelated issues.

These families' experiences underscore the notion that better management and coordination across institutions will not rectify the existing inequalities; in many ways, they only serve to amplify them. This phenomenon can be seen in the criminal justice system, where the shift in traditional processing of misdemeanor offenses to a managerial one (Kohler-Hausmann 2018) further penalizes low-level offenders. The increased use of risk assessments based on "objective" algorithms to determine bail decisions for adults or programming options for youths in the juvenile justice system do not help predict better outcomes as much as they encode existing racial, class, and gender inequalities in the justice system and society more generally (Picard et al. 2019).[6] Similarly, in the welfare arena, the recent efforts in the United Kingdom to streamline its welfare benefits into one system have led to delays in financial payments that propel families further into debt.[7] In short, these attempts at improved management and coordination appear only good at getting families into the maze—not necessarily to get them out of it.

More Focus on the Accountability of Institutions, Not of Families

Finally, we need to shift the analytical and policy gaze from individual families' efforts more onto the systemic issues impeding those families from becoming self-sufficient. In that sense, the focus of change lies not only on the individuals who participate in these programs but also on the systems that shape the conditions that compel those programs to exist. Going back to Leisy's SSI experience, how could the institutional processes have gone more smoothly without leading to more institutional involvements for her family? One way to answer that question is to look at what Herd and Moynihan call "administrative burdens," or "the learning, psychological, and compliance costs that citizens experience in their interactions with government" (2018: 22).[8] This multifaceted view of a burden encompasses both "official" rules and policies, alongside individuals' experience of those rules. Herd and Moynihan argue that if we don't know what those burdens are, any policy reform effort will be limited in effect, as it fails to address the three types of costs (i.e., learning, compliance, and psychological) to the individuals affected by that policy.[9] This is especially true if the policy makers and reformers have not themselves experienced those policies; they might propose a "logical" change to the system based on some management principle without anticipating how people might respond in a different way than intended due to one or all of those costs. Herd and Moynihan write that programs should be "simple, their processes accessible and respectful to the people they encounter" (2018: 257). They describe such a shift in an innovative tax filing program in California, where the tax agency determines an individual's tax liability or refund and sends its evaluation to that individual. If the individual agrees, she signs the form. That speeds up the process, decreases the number of staff needed, and also reduces the number of errors, as the agency already gets the income information from the companies.

Simply put, the focus, then, should be on what institutions are doing, versus on what families are doing. That would enable us to change the discourse about the poor or those who are economically struggling from being "dependent" or "part of the "welfare culture," to what Duflo and Banerjee (2019) see as "society's fallen heroes."[10] But it is more than just being society's fallen heroes. Poor families are most affected by societal disruptions and fall prey to government policies that do not fully intend to help them but also do not fully desert them. In short, it is social institutions that have failed the families, not the families who have failed in not being able to meet the requirements of those institutions. Put another way, the institutions create the walls in the maze, with families left to figure out how to survive within it.

RECONSIDERING INSTITUTIONS' INTERVENTIONS

What might have the institutions done differently for these families? This book ends by offering five specific policy recommendations. The recommendations are more practically oriented and feasible than the more fundamental reforms such as Medicare for All or Universal Basic Income.[11] At the same time, I do not mean to suggest that such fundamental reforms should be seen as impossible; rather, I mean that as we continue to fight for those goals, the incremental reforms posed here might help us get there and, in the meantime, can improve families' lives right now.[12]

1. Rethink the Timing and Frequency of "Intakes" and "Treatment Plans"

It seems an obvious point that people might not be forthright in providing all the relevant information during the first meeting with institutional staff; just like one would not share with a person she just met in everyday life. In this study, families only opened up to me after several months of hanging out and on their own timeframes. That is, I didn't explicitly ask them about those experiences; families mentioned them organically on their own. Yet much of institutions' work is based on such a requirement as they are set up for assessing families at the onset, either to provide a more comprehensive plan or to withhold resources for gatekeeping purposes. Instead, we need to figure out a way to get information about families' unique institutional histories over time with enough flexibility in the institutional processes to change course in action, based on that information.

Another reason to rethink how institutions conduct assessments pertains to the scope of those questions. We often do not think to ask about a past institutional encounter or another family member as relevant to the specific institutional matter at hand. Yet they do matter. For example, while doctors don't often think to ask about past family histories of other illnesses, this book has showed how a previous hospitalization for one family member's illness shapes her approach to her child's treatment for another disease.

So instead of putting so much emphasis on establishing a plan at the front end of services, I propose that institutions reconsider the timing and scope of their assessment process. It is not about redesigning the intake questionnaire to ask about all possible institutional experiences (e.g., check all that apply). Rather, one could do a "check-in" session every few months to ask families how else the institution could assist or facilitate the family's needs. It could address if there are any new developments or issues the family wanted to share with the staff that would help them work toward that goal. In those meetings, staff would be open to how the families talk about their institutional experiences. That knowledge would assist staff's efforts in achieving a more effective and integrated interagency approach. In my fieldwork, being attuned to those sometimes off-handed comments helped me make connections between seemingly unrelated institutional experiences. To be more intentional and respectful in this endeavor, staff might consider asking families general questions about their day or week (e.g., "What did you do this week? Did you have any meetings?") with language that does not sound so formal or institutional (e.g., "experiences" versus "cases," "troubles" versus "conflict," "expectations" versus "compliance") to avoid alienating or disempowering families. Moreover, those conversations are not just about the family's compliance or progress to date, they present an opportunity to include family evaluations of the institution's efforts as well.

2. Rethink the Idea of Family Advocates

Currently, family advocates exist in individual institutions (e.g., hospitals, child welfare) to help families navigate those particular systems. This idea would broaden that role across multiple institutions but in a reimagined way. The family advocate first would spend time with the family in an informal way, getting a sense of its needs as discussed in the previous point. Yet in contrast to the current form of these advocates, this position would not be affiliated with any one institution. That lack of affiliation would help build rapport with the family by avoiding the negative associations that a family might have with an institution. An even better option would be a person whom the family identifies in its own network, circle, or community. If they can't think of anyone, a volunteer from a community organization could serve in that role. The advocates would be able to talk to the institutions about what is relevant or ask the families if they could speak on their behalf (or encourage them to do it themselves). The purpose of this position is to help, not further penalize, families. Training would be imperative here to help that person know the appropriate issues regarding confidentiality and all the systems (or point people in those systems) that they can reach out to in order to find the suitable responses to the family's issues.[13]

3. Incorporate Judicious Nonintervention in the Multi-Institutional Context

Implementing this concept of limiting the punitive influences of institutions in families' lives helps ensure that families are not lured into an endless web of bureaucracy where each additional "administrative burden" (Herd and Moynihan 2018) could lead to more feelings of frustration and possibly insufficient help.[14] This is not about gatekeeping or withholding resources in the social welfare agencies. It is more about recognizing that families' experiences with even "helping" institutions can affect their subsequent decisions about approaching the same institutions in future situations—where they do qualify but might not seek help.[15] In the case of the more punishment-oriented institutions, where the interventions are supposed to "encourage" or "strongarm" them into subservience, this principle is even more important if the institution further penalizes them in subsequent interactions, not just for that institution but for others (e.g., a failure in a court diversion program leading a loss of housing benefits based on the person's "felon" status).

Part of determining whether to intervene or not is to try to foresee a path forward for the family—again, realizing one cannot know everything in advance. If there are not clear pathways out of the institutional intervention, such as when a delinquency court is faced with a family whose youth has significant mental health issues (e.g., Talia's family), then perhaps it is best to not start the process at all. Another way to think about the path is to do a cost-benefit analysis of the intervention; again, if the costs appear to outweigh the benefits, perhaps it would be best to not do anything. By *costs*, I refer to the impacts on family (financially, socially, and psychologically) and to the institutions (resources to allocate to the family relative to others).

It also involves greater transparency in what it means to open a case and which institutions are involved in that case. Also, there should be clearer lines between public and private institutions that are subcontracted to provide some component of that public service. My work on fines and fees in the juvenile justice system (Paik and Packard 2019) shows that families get deeper into debt with each court decision aimed at "helping" youths learn responsibility, mainly because the families don't know about the fees associated with such programs. So, in this regard, institutions need to convey clearly to families up front about these types of costs or obligations before and during the process.

4. Shorten the Timeframe That Institutions Work with Families If It Seems the Case Will Not Be Resolved

Building off the prior three points, any open case should be reevaluated on a continual basis—by both staff and families—as to whether it is going to be resolved. If it appears that the institutions do not have the resources or capacity to help the families in those situations, they should set a firm timeframe to close the case to avoid a situation that further stigmatizes and penalizes families. This idea is not meant to be applied to interventions such as public assistance, Medicaid, or housing assistance, upon which families rely for basic support. For those institutions, it would be important to reduce the threats to continued support such as eliminating time limits to TANF (Temporary Assistance for Needy Families) if the available jobs are not economically viable. Rather, I mean lingering surveilling types of interventions such as child welfare in which the institution cannot adequately provide services to resolve a family's conflicts, as in Talia and Catherine's families. Instead of marking these outcomes as client failures, they should be recorded as administrative discharges or more specifically, instances of institutional mismatch, that do not carry any negative penalty on the family. This would provide more exits or "off-ramps" out of the maze rather than creating more entry points for the family.

If we think about those instances of institutional mismatch more intentionally, they can help expose the changing needs of families in contemporary times and how we can begin to realign the institutions with families. This would be similar to what Herd and Moynihan discuss regarding administrative burdens (2018), which should not be used to call for the end of services but to inform improvements to those programs.[16]

5. Focus on Family Agency in Process

Finally, and perhaps most importantly, we need to shift the power dynamics between institutions and families to be more equal with one another. Instead of institutions trying to control or compel families to do what we think they should do, they should create a greater role and spot at the table for families in which the staff's role would be to, as Cottam writes, " step back . . . and ask the families themselves to solve the conundrum" (2018: 877).[17] Increased family agency could mean that families would do continual evaluations of the staff's performance and inform the discussions about whether to set a firm deadline to close the case in situations of institutional mismatch as discussed in the previous point. They also could interview potential candidates to select their "advocates" among an approved group of people from the community agencies. These newfound roles for families in their institutional involvements would give them a greater sense of control over the process and help establish a rapport and trust with the staff across institutions.

What would greater family voices mean in this more informal and creative setting that focuses on building the family's capabilities? Leisy had housing and health care but was fighting with Supplemental Security Income for disability benefits. Instead of continually assessing her mental health issues with the "court-approved" doctors and paperwork, perhaps we should be asking, "what would it take to support Leisy in her attempts to work while also taking into consideration her mental health issues?" One approach would be to encourage her to volunteer while getting partial disability benefits and then building up her skillset to qualify for a more permanent job that can accommodate her mental health issues.[18] For example, Leisy expressed several times to me that she wanted to improve her technological literacy, from using her phone to learning how to type and use the internet. We once went to sign her up for computer classes at the local library, which she had to miss due to her many appointments, which she had no control over scheduling. I could imagine a scenario in which Leisy volunteers at the library while also taking computer classes there, gaining the skills needed to apply for entry-level clerical jobs. Similarly, Talia supports her family with housing benefits and public assistance. She also had several ideas for businesses and was constantly trying to learn new things on the internet. Perhaps we could help her think about what kinds of jobs would be viable for her many and varied skills, whether it is a small business of her own or to work for a small company based on her interests. Finally, Catherine is perhaps the most successful member of my families in terms of work. She consistently increased her hours and skills as an outreach HIV worker to the point where she was almost working full-time. However, no matter how many hours she got from her job, it would not be sufficient to cover her health care costs if the agency did not provide adequate insurance. If those health benefits were separate, she would perhaps be able to do more work—which she enjoys and takes great pride in doing—and rely less on other benefit programs such as food stamps.

In sum, we should be asking ourselves and public institutions the following questions: What do families want or need? What are they willing to do? What are they able to do? What can agencies do to help them get there? What would be our responses if agencies can't help or if families don't get there? Asking those questions will enable us to come up with creative and long-term plans that seek permanent and positive change for the families. Those changes benefit not just the individual family but also the community (e.g., greater potential civic participation by the family, greater public safety in cases of youth delinquency, and less police resources spent on responding to mental health issues) and society more broadly (e.g., less government expenditures spent on family, greater workforce participation for parents, and better outcomes for the children).

In closing, we should ask ourselves what we hope to achieve in our efforts to fight poverty. As part of that discussion, we should critically reflect upon the continued distinctions such as the deserving and undeserving poor, as well as entitlement-based and social rights. The enduring trope of the "undeserving" poor perpetuates social inequalities and leads to greater levels of distrust in government among those disenfranchised populations. While it does provide political benefit to conservatives and other critics of government spending, it does not save the government significant amounts of money compared to its spending in other budget categories (e.g., military, tax cuts for businesses). And if in fact, entitlement programs do benefit the larger society, why are they stigmatized while social programs such as Medicare and Social Security are not?[19] Seeing them as stabilizing situations for the most disadvantaged for the good of us all is key to the future of these programs' vitality. We are all just one step away from needing assistance and will draw from the government at some point in our lives, whether it is for immediate needs, chronic illness, or retirement benefits. So, instead of pitting groups of people against one another, it would be more productive to work collectively to demand government programs that support all families, in whatever form they may take.

Postscript

Brief Update about the Families

I have been in touch with six of the families in the ethnography through Facebook or occasional phone calls since the study ended.[1] Gigi and Sulia Hernandez continue to live with Sulia's parents in the same apartment; as it was a relatively short phone call that focused on the book's themes, I wasn't able to ask more about what Gigi was doing since high school. Three families (Fouskases, Velezes, and Thomases) moved out of state, two of which went down south. Eileen Fouskas moved to Florida with her youngest son and is working in childcare; she is in a relationship as well. Lita Velez and her family moved full-time to Pennsylvania to be near one of her sisters, after Julio retired from his job. They kept their apartment in New York (which is technically under her brother's name) so they can come back to get their medical care and for Lita to be able to check on her brother. Christine has not yet started college but says she plans to start in August. She is now nineteen years old and working. Matthew just started high school in Pennsylvania.

Below I present two families' updates in more depth—the Bryants and the Thomases—one of whom stayed in New York and the other who left.

CATHERINE BRYANT AND TALIA THOMAS: MARRIAGE AND MOVING TO OPPORTUNITY?

I visited Catherine Bryant about six months after our fieldwork period ended. She was about to get married, living across the street from her apartment with her fiancé and Rodney in his one-bedroom apartment; her fiancé was a veteran with several health problems requiring a full-time home health aide. Edward was transferred to a group home upstate (about four and a half hours away) for eighteen months; he had some behavioral issues that prolonged his stay but started doing better after his family came to visit him. Rodney was in first grade and doing well academically albeit with some occasional fighting; the school doubled his ADHD medication. Her three older granddaughters (Latisha, Alisha, and Tori) stayed in her apartment. They were working toward finishing high school; the oldest, Latisha, hopes to finish in January. She said Latisha was looking for a job but needed to get a state ID, which is being held up because she first needs to get a birth certificate. Their mother, Tanisha, and her boyfriend and baby moved into an apartment that used to be her brother's (Edward's dad) after he moved to New Jersey. Tanisha is not working and has not yet signed up for welfare; her boyfriend has signed up for it and put the baby on his case. Her other three children live with their father. Catherine and Edward's dad are talking but there is still tension there. Edward's dad is having another baby and told Edward that if he doesn't live with him after he gets out of the facility (which Edward doesn't want to do), he will have no contact with the baby. Edward's older brother still lives in the South with his mother. Catherine's life seemed stable and economically stronger due to her husband's and her combined income. However, her husband passed away within a year, after which I lost touch.

Talia Thomas moved out of state with her younger children (Aliyah, Mia, and another baby she had with her boyfriend, Darnell). Darnell and Talia broke up; she subsequently reconciled with Michael, but he passed away a year later. Talia found out she was not entitled to his death benefits because they were not legally married. Her two older sons, MJ and Samuel, stayed in New York. MJ is going to college upstate, working in human resources and living with his girlfriend. Samuel initially appeared to be doing well, working and living with his girlfriend but eventually started having problems. Talia claims he still has mental health issues that are not fully treated; she says he turned to using drugs to get rid of his thoughts. As he is an adult now, she can't force him to get treatment. Last time she heard from him, he was living in and out of homeless shelters. She still blames the juvenile court for not intervening when she asked. She also says her housing court and child welfare case technically are still open because she was never able to get back to New York to close them successfully. Due to the open child welfare case, she claims she cannot become a foster mom or a parent advocate, both of which she says she wants to do.

Methods and Reflexivity

The idea for this project came out of my first book (2011) when I saw how different the staff and families' views of parental involvement in their teenagers' court cases could be. So much was left unsaid, misinterpreted, or discovered only after the fact, especially given that notions of youth and parent responsibility changed over time and shaped their actions regarding the youth's case. For this project, I initially began looking at family involvement in courts from the family perspective, only to realize I could not do so in isolation. Rather the involvement was shaped by families' experiences in other institutions. I was struck again and again by how many parents and youths alike referred to the staff from various institutions as a collective, "they," whether they were police, social workers, or teachers, often not distinguishing them by affiliation but rather, as a similar type of omnipotent presence in their lives. With that simple word use, I began to pay more attention to how families viewed and interacted with these institutions, beyond just the individual case at hand.

Because the study started with a focus on family involvement in their teenagers' cases, I recruited families whose youths were involved in three organizations: two court diversion agencies dealing with youths who had delinquency cases and a hospital treating youths with chronic illnesses in New York City. I previously had worked with one of the diversion agencies' head organization, so I got access through those connections. The hospital was affiliated with my university, so I was able to obtain access through the dean of the medical school. After getting IRB approval for the study, I asked these organizations to pass flyers along to prospective families, either by mail or, if appropriate, in their one-on-one meetings. They also posted those flyers in their waiting rooms.

My research assistants and I accompanied the hospital staff to local health fairs and community events where we passed out the flyers to potential families. In this recruitment process, I described the study as a project that sought to better understand their experiences in those two respective institutions, particularly in how those institutions affected their family life and vice versa.

I collected the data in two phases: I first conducted one-time interviews from 2011 to 2013 with thirty parents whose youths had active delinquency cases in Family Court and an in-depth ethnography and follow-up interviews with four of those families over twelve months from 2013 to 2014. Working with a local hospital, I interviewed parents and youths from another thirty-three families from 2015 to 2016; I also started conducting an in-depth ethnography and follow-up interviews with six of those families for at least twelve months from 2015 to 2017. For the ethnographic sample, I selected families based mainly on their willingness to continue their participation past the initial interview for another year; for the families whom I recruited through the hospital, I specifically tried to obtain some variation in the medical conditions of the youths.[1] In between visits and interviews, I kept in touch via phone, email, and text with the families in ethnography, particularly the families of Catherine, Eileen, Jessica, Michelle, and Viola. Those communications helped me keep abreast of what was happening even if I wasn't there. In total, 134 interviews and 140 ethnographic visits were completed.

The ethnography portion of this study was important to capture the families' experiences of the multi-institutional maze. Spending time with families over the course of a year or longer, I was able to get a better sense of how they manage institutional expectations in real time, as well as how those institutional conditions shape their interactions with each other (e.g., creating tension between parent and child) and vice versa. Moreover, those moments of just "hanging out" with family allowed for more organic conversations about their past institutional experiences and how they made connections between those and their current ones. I do not think I could have gotten that kind of information in the one-time interviews, given that I would not have had the same level of trust and rapport with the families and the families would have had to think on the spot about those connections (which came out more in the moment during my visits).

I paid families for their participation in this project. For those whom I recruited through the court diversion agencies, I paid $20 or $50 for the one-time interviews with the parents; I paid an additional $465 to the four families in the ethnography. For the families recruited through the hospital, I paid families a total of $70 for the one-time interviews with the parents and youths ($50 to parents and $20 to youths); for the six families in the ethnography, I paid an additional $600. The amounts for the one-time interviews differed due to the policies of the recruiting agencies; one asked that I pay parents $20 instead of my typical amount of $50. Regarding the differing amounts for the ethnographies, I paid more to the families I recruited from the hospital setting, as I wanted to do more observations with them, given my lack of previous research on health-related institutional involvements. In the end, I did seven to twelve visits with the court-involved families and fourteen to twenty-one visits with the health-involved ones.

As mentioned in the first chapter, I had research assistants to help with the data collection and analysis portion of the project. Over the course of the study, two masters and three undergraduate students (one Latina, two Latino, and two African American) did some of the interviews and ethnographic visits. I always had a Spanish-speaking research assistant to help me with the Spanish-only speaking parents. While I have a basic comprehension of Spanish, I cannot easily converse on my own. That did limit the level of rapport that I was able to have with those families to some extent and also shaped who was in the ethnographic study, as there was only one Spanish-speaking family in it (the Cabreras), even though the father spoke English and the mother understood English. During the coding process of the health interviews, I also hired a white female sociology doctoral student to help me supervise two research assistants doing some of the interview coding.

BACKGROUND INFORMATION ABOUT THE FAMILIES

In comparison to the general New York City population, the families in my sample had a slightly higher household size. According to the US Census Bureau's (2017) American Community Survey (ACS),[2] the average family size in the city was 3.5; the average in my sample was 4.1. Regarding family structure, 37 percent of my sample were two-parent households (including stepparent/parent), 51 percent were single parents and 13 percent were extended kin.[3]

My sample contains a larger representation of Latinx (50%) and Black (36%) families compared to the general New York City population in 2017 (29%[4] and 24%, respectively) as measured by the ACS. As shown in Table A, it also has higher rates of Latinx and Black families compared to the racial breakdown of the poor in New York City in 2017 from two different sources: ACS and the City government which use two different measures of poverty.[5]

The racial differences in my sample to the ACS and New York City government data make sense when considering the overrepresentation of poor Black and Latinx families in the juvenile justice system and racial disparities in health, the two issues I focused on at the onset of this study. Using unpublished data provided by the New York State Division of Criminal Justice Services, Citizens' Committee for Children found that of the 29,650 delinquency arrests in New York City from 2011 to 2013, 58.2 percent were for Black youths, 32.8 percent Latinx, and 5.3 percent white.[6] Minority poor youths have higher rates of asthma, obesity, and diabetes compared to their white middle/upper class counterparts. Schwarz et al. (2008) found that 12 percent of Hispanic and 10 percent Black children, ages 0–17, have asthma compared to 4 percent of whites; in 2003, 320,000 youths had been diagnosed with asthma, 170,000 had an attack or episode within the last year. Day et al. (2014) also found racial differences for obesity among public school students in grades K–8 with 25.6 percent Hispanic, 20.9 percent Black, 15.4 percent white, and 13.4 percent Asians meeting that criteria.[7] Finally, Wallach and Rey (2009) found that Hispanic and Black youths in New York City were more likely to be obese compared to their white and Asian counterparts, increasing their risk of developing type 2 diabetes.

TABLE A   FAMILIES WITH CHILDREN UNDER EIGHTEEN BY RACE

Race/Ethnicity	Families in My Sample %	ACS % of Poor Families in NYC	NYC.gov % Poor Families in NYC
Hispanic	50	41[a]	22.6
Black	36	28	20.9
Non-Hispanic white	6	19	12.5
Asian	0	13	24.9
Some other race or two/more races	8	24	

a. This percentage is for Hispanic or Latino origin of any race. As such, the percentages in this column exceed 100% as it combines race and Hispanic/Latino origin. Data is from the ACS Table S1701, "Poverty Status in the Past 12 Months."

Extrapolating from these comparisons, I think it is reasonable to say that the families in my sample generally reflect the population of families in New York City who are involved in the institutions discussed in this book. While other poor minority families may not be involved in as many institutions, I argue that the experiences of my families in the multi-institutional maze would resonate with those families, even if in a more limited fashion.[8]

ESTABLISHING AND BUILDING RAPPORT WITH THE PARENTS AND YOUTHS

Building rapport with the families took time and varied greatly among the parents and youths. In some ways, I connected with parents by openly recognizing my different social position as a middle-class Asian woman with no children; I expressed my sincere awe and respect in their efforts to raise teenagers amid all these institutional struggles. I also would bring food (or cook food together), and send birthday cards and occasional greeting cards to help build the connection between the family and me, which helped strengthen my relationship with the youths and parents. Finally, I think for many families, our shared religious beliefs helped to connect us; when I asked parents to whom they turned for support in the initial interviews, many mentioned turning to God for emotional support. At that point, I would share with them that I was also a person of faith and that if they were okay with it, I would be praying for them (which I did) as one way to support them.

My connections with the youths overall were not as strong as my relationships with the parents. I did the majority of the data collection with the youths and spent significant amounts of time with a few, going with them on their commutes from school to home or just hanging out with them individually at their homes. But my research assistants played a key role with the youths as well, given that they were closer in age with the youths. It also helped that most of them also grew up in New York City and attended public schools there, so they could at least start with that basic level of rapport and build with similar interests in movies, music, and popular culture. In most cases, I matched the research assistants to youths of the same race and gender. I had the research assistants spend time alone with the youths to get their perspective while I focused on the parents, either during the home visits or alone where they took them out for pizza or the movies. In comparing our fieldnotes, my research assistants did get some more information about the youth's daily lives (including activities that they might not have shared with an adult like me) but not necessarily anything that helped inform my understanding about their family's institutional involvements. That being said, I think the parents saw my research assistants as quasi–role models for their youths as people who had graduated from similar high schools and were pursuing college and graduate degrees; this strengthened our overall rapport with the families.

RETURNING TO THE FIELD

I reached out to the ten families in the ethnography as I was writing up the results to get their feedback on the book.[9] I used Facebook, letters and phone calls if I still had their phone number (I left general messages for a couple which had an automated voicemail so I couldn't confirm it was still their number). I discussed the book's findings and general outline with four families. All were fine with the outline of the book and their part in it. While I made contact with two other families, we were never able to schedule a time to discuss the book in detail.

REFLEXIVITY

Doing an ethnography is equal parts exhilarating, exhausting, and exasperating.

It is exhilarating to get to know these families after building up enough rapport and trust to be allowed into their lives; moreover, the difficulties in scheduling time with the families made each home visit and interview feel like a precious hard-earned gift. Doing this kind of ethnography is exhausting— both physically and emotionally, in having to get in touch (and back in touch) with the families, matching the families' availability to those of my research assistants and me, traveling back and forth to all the neighborhoods on public transportation and most importantly, seeing the families go through the multi-institutional maze in front of our eyes. Finally, conducting ethnographic research can be exasperating as I tried to manage all of those issues at the same time while knowing I was not in control of any of them.

Below are five methodological challenges that I encountered doing this project.

1. Managing Logistics

The practical issues in doing this kind of research are so numerous that to present them all is far beyond the scope of this appendix. While it seems that doing a minimum of seven to fourteen ethnographic visits to each family over at least twelve months should not be that difficult to arrange, it was much more complicated than meets the eye. Time-wise, I would have to spend three to four hours round-trip in travel on public transportation to catch a court hearing or see a family just for an hour. For every visit I completed, there were several cancellations, as families would call to reschedule, or long delays in between visits, as they would fall out of touch with phone numbers going out of service or letters going unanswered. I did find that texting or messaging via Facebook was a great way to keep in touch with families. They didn't really like to talk on the phone, and I think for some, it was an issue of saving their minutes to not go over the allotted amount on their monthly plan.

For many families, weeks sometimes went by before I got in touch with anyone. If it had been over a month, I would drop by their homes for an in-person visit, even if it was not scheduled. Sometimes those drop-in visits felt futile if they weren't home. Other times, they were happy to see me, saying I was welcome any time. One family kept asking me "where have you been?" when the reality was, I was constantly calling and mailing them letters, but they kept changing their phone number and not responding to my letters. While I was frustrated and wanted to say that they did not respond to me, I simply smiled to say that I know it has been a long time and that I was happy to see them again.

The time spent in scheduling these visits meant I would have to keep many days free just on the chance that they would call. While this felt like a lot of time wasted, I believe it helped me build rapport with the families who saw that they had control over the scheduling process, versus being at the mercy of my schedule. In this way, I was able to separate myself from the institutions that demanded their presence, sometimes with little advance notice. I also recognized that the families were busy and dealing with a lot of things. I didn't want to harass them or add to their stress with constant calls to ask to schedule a visit. Regarding the travel time to and from appointments, I found it helped me to get a better sense of the families' daily struggles in getting to multiple appointments across the city; on a practical note, the long commutes on public transportation provided dedicated time for me to write up my fieldnotes right after each visit and get my thoughts down while they were fresh.

2. Balancing Researcher-Friend Role with Parents and Youth

I sometimes struggled with my role with the families. I felt at times that I was the only confidante to some mothers; while they all had friends and lots of family nearby, they also said they didn't really talk to them about their youths' cases or issues, similar to the instances of "social poverty" found in Halpern-Meekin's study (2019). Some wanted me to do social activities with them; I always said no to help maintain the boundaries. I also was very clear to remind them that I was a researcher, not a friend. When I called, I always said, "This is Leslie from City College" or when I sent greeting cards, I included my business card. I would routinely remind them that I was going to write up the results from the study and that I would share a generalized summary of my findings with them if they wanted. Again, I am not sure entirely how they viewed me or presented our connection to others; but I did see these small reminders and clarifications as ways to maintain the boundaries between the participants and me.

3. *Knowing When to Intervene or Not*

A related and even more difficult dilemma to navigate was intervening in the families' cases. As a researcher, I was supposed to observe how they themselves understood the issue and navigated through the maze. As an empathetic person who wanted to help, I yearned to give advice when parents would describe their view about their situation if I thought I could offer a more effective strategy. I constantly was trying to reconcile those two perspectives with each family and with each situation. Below are three instances that exemplified situations that came up regularly while doing the fieldwork.

A. I Could Help You . . .

Perhaps the most complicated issue was when I thought of a concrete way to help the family get through at least one part of the maze. Do I tell them that idea or wait to see how the family navigates on its own? My rationale in deciding when to offer help was twofold: when it would directly benefit the person's health or situation in tangible ways and if I could not see another possible way for the person to get the same response. For example, Gigi kept telling me over months that she was sad and couldn't stop sleeping. Dr. Peters mentioned to me in a prior conversation that her fatigue could be a symptom of possible depression and a delayed reaction to her diabetes diagnosis. I knew that even though she had her own health insurance card to make appointments, Gigi would not initiate seeking mental health treatment on her own because her mom made all her appointments for her. So, I first asked Gigi if she minded if I spoke with Dr. Peters about the possibility of getting counseling for her. Once she said it was okay, I talked it over with Dr. Peters who printed out a referral for her that she could use any time. I then gave it to her during one of our one-on-one visits, saying it was completely up to her to use it to seek out the treatment on her own. This response felt like the appropriate middle ground where I didn't ignore her potential pleas for help but also still preserved her agency in the process by first asking her permission to talk with the doctor and to give her the referral to use when she wanted to do so.

B. Sorting Out Paperwork

Paperwork played a big role in shaping how the families' cases were processed. While listening to the parents talk about the paperwork, I often had to resist the urge to offer to review the forms with them. I only looked at the documents when families showed them to me or asked me something specific about them. As discussed in chapter 3, Talia did ask me once to help her sort through papers regarding her housing court case. That was a humbling exercise for me to learn what parents go through with these multi-institutional involvements. There was incomplete or missing information from the welfare agency, data that wasn't easily reconciled between welfare and housing court, and an overall ambiguity in processes. I started to try to write out how much each agency was paying and what was outstanding. While it still wasn't complete, it did provide us both with a better sense of what she needed to do. Going back to my policy recommendation in the conclusion, I often wondered what it would take for a family advocate to be effective in this situation: beyond helping Talia go through the information, the advocate would need to (1) know the situation existed, with (2) enough time and the authority to get that information from the relevant agencies, to be able then to (3) assist and advise Talia on how to navigate these systems.

C. Who Are You? Talking to Institutions

Going with the families to medical and court appointments raised another set of issues regarding how I would present my relationship with them to the staff and how I would act in those interactions. The parents often told staff that I was their friend. I would say I am doing a project trying to understand family involvement in their youths' cases. Sometimes the staff would know who I was if they referred the family to me. But even if they didn't, the staff were fine with me sitting in the appointments as long as the family said it was okay. If I was observing the court hearings, I sometimes did not state who I was if I came separately from the family; Family Court in New York City is open to the public, in which case I told the bailiffs that I just wanted to observe the cases in general. If someone asked specifically why I was there, I would say that I am a sociology professor interested in how the court works. I would not identify the families as being part of the study because I did not want to do anything to compromise their youths' cases that were still open. Most of the time, I didn't say anything in any of these encounters, observing how the families talked with the staff and what happened.

However, there were a few times where I did more than disclose my connection to the families. As discussed in chapter 2, Leisy had an appointment to appeal for Kobe's SSI benefits being reinstated. It was in downtown Manhattan, an area that she did not know well. It was at least an hour ride by subway from the Bronx. As she was running extremely late due to another prior appointment that she could not reschedule, I did go up to the officer to ask what might happen if she missed her appointment time (which she did). The letter stated that if she was late, she would not be granted another appointment. Once she got to the building over an hour after her appointment time, understandably nervous about what might happen, I told her that we'd go to the office and see. At that point, I did offer to talk with the staff as she was out of sorts and couldn't really explain herself very clearly. I also called a number that the staff provided to talk with someone on her behalf to try to reschedule the appointment. While I clearly did more "participating" than "observing" in that instance, I believed that it was more ethical to help the family in these specific moments, where it visibly could improve their situation in material or emotional ways.

In all these situations, I had to remind myself that I was not a social worker, counselor or their friend; rather my job was to depict the families' lives with as much honesty and dignity as I could so others could see the challenges that they face on a daily basis. That reminder kept me grounded when I felt like I could do nothing to help them with any problems or frustrations they might be having, beyond those crisis moments mentioned above. I also realized that it was incredibly presumptuous of me to think I would know how to do it better or more effectively. More often than not, it was enough for parents to know I was on their side to listen and walk alongside them on their incredibly difficult journeys in the maze.

4. Recognizing the Emotional Toll

Finally, I vastly underestimated the emotional impact that this kind of fieldwork would have on me. It is one thing to go to the courtrooms and hear the individuals' stories in one-time interviews as in my previous work (2011); it is quite another to spend time in families' homes, which often are overcrowded and not well maintained by the landlords, and to see them battle what feels like the constant assault of poverty and racism over several visits. Listening to their stories about past and current involvements also was its own kind of trauma, or what my therapist at the time referred to as "secondary trauma." While it certainly is not the same as what the families experienced, secondary trauma is not something that I could ignore or rationalize away as meaningless either. I learned in this project that breaks for self-care are crucial while doing fieldwork. Taking long walks, getting regular exercise, going to hear some music or whatever might help you get out of your head for a while—these short respites are necessary and restorative, enabling the ethnographer to continue on with the fieldwork.

5. Focusing on Families' Accounts

I focused on families' accounts of their experiences (Scott and Lyman 1968), versus trying to obtain a "factual" verification of their cases. In many ways, we often rely too much on the official record when in fact it is the families' own understanding of their experiences that should be prioritized—that is, the families' actions depend on how they view the situation, not what "really" is the situation. This focus leads to a sticky situation when I couldn't always trust what the family was telling me about their institutional involvements. Since I was trying to see the family's situation from their perspective, I did not want to appear to be questioning their statements. On a practical and ethical note, I also could not just call up any institution to see if I could access the family's records or talk to the staff working on their cases. At the same time, I couldn't just accept everything that the family said as fact. Rather, it is important to be skeptical when things don't make sense to you and those things are central to understand for your study. In those situations, I tried to find people or other sources to ask about the subjects' story, whether a family member, family friend, or staff person working with the family—whoever I was allowed to talk to under the IRB.[10]

When I started interviews in 2011, I could not have envisioned that this project, which started initially as a simple attempt to understand family involvement in juvenile court, would balloon into this book about multi-institutional involvement. At the same time, one of the strengths of fieldwork is the openness to seeing members' meanings (Emerson, Fretz, and Shaw 1995); that basic principle allowed me to broaden my perspective about poor families' institutional involvement and by extension, hopefully yours as well.

List of Families

Family Last Name	Parents in Study (age)	Household Structure	Race/ Ethnicity of Parents	Children (ages) Italicized in Household	Currently Working FT: Full-Time PT: Part-Time (* if middle class)
Aguilar	Miraya (45)	Single	Latinx	*Arlene (15)*	Y-PT
Anderson	Marsha (36)	Single	Black	*George (15), Malcolm (13)*	N
Barnes	Carla (40)	Two-parent— married/stepdad	Other	*Al (22), Nathan (19), Brady (15)*	N
Bryant	Catherine (51)	Extended kin— grandmother	Black	*Shawn (15), Edward (13), Rodney (5)*	Y-PT
Cabrera	Sofia (44) & Diego (48)	Two-parent— married	Latinx	Henry (21), *Mark (19) Richard (16)*	Y-FT
Campbell	Regina (33)	Single	Black	*Ally (13), Caleb (16)*	N
Carter	Sally (70)	Extended kin— grandparents	Black	Daughter, *Nicole (16), grandson*	N*

Family Last Name	Parents in Study (age)	Household Structure	Race/ Ethnicity of Parents	Children (ages) Italicized in Household	Currently Working FT: Full-Time PT: Part-Time (* if middle class)
Castillo	Paula (46)	Single	Latinx	Gina (26), Jovanny (26), *Emilio (15)*	Y-FT
Chavez	Antonella (46)	Single	Latinx	*Gael (15)*	Y-FT
Cole	Rody (38)	Two-parent— married	Black	*Sports (12), Larissa (14), Daniel (5), Vivian (5), Dule (6)*	N
Cruz	Adriana (44)	Two-parent— married	Latinx	Angel (27), *Danna (16), 2 sons and 1 daughter (23, 21, 1.5), grandchild*	N
Delgado	Josefina (49)	Two-parent— married	Latinx	*Nhazul (15), 1 son and 2 daughters (19, 17, 13)*	Y-PT
Desoto	Claudia (52)	Single	Latinx	Natalia (29), *Miguel (15)*	Y-FT
Diaz	Veronica (35)	Single	Latinx	*Mateo (14)*	N
Elliot	Melissa (44)	Two-parent— married	Black	*Evelyn (14)*	Y-FT*
Evans	Ethel (52)	Extended kin— aunt	Black	*Micah (16), Shontae (14)*	N
Flores	Emilia (41)	Single	Latinx	*Melanie (14), 2 sons and 1 daughter (4, 5, 9)*	Y-PT
Fouskas	Eileen (45)	Single	White	Joey (22), Patrick (13), *Brian (10)*	N
Garcia	Gabriela (24)	Two-parent— married	Latinx	*Bianca (13), Emmanuel (17), Liam(11), Noa (8), Sofia (3)*	Y-FT (dad)

Family Last Name	Parents in Study (age)	Household Structure	Race/ Ethnicity of Parents	Children (ages) Italicized in Household	Currently Working FT: Full-Time PT: Part-Time (* if middle class)
Garner	Viola (54)	Two-parent— married/stepdad	Black	Jay (28), Jim (20), Xavier (26), *Annette (16), Star (14)*	N
Garza	Rosa (53)	Two-parent— married/stepmom	Latinx	3 sons, *Benicio (20) Oliver (15) José (15), Clara (13)*	N
Gray	Salome (50)	Two-parent— married/stepdad	Other	Althia, *Mara (13)*	Y-PT
Gutierrez	Aprendiendo (36)	Two-parent— married	Latinx	*Bob (16), Olivia (9)*	Y-PT
Guzman	Fabiana (37)	Single	Latinx	Luca (15), *Julian (9)*	Y-FT
Hernandez	Sulia (45)	Single (live with parents)	Latinx	Katy (25), *Gigi (16), Aracely (14), Isaiah (10)*	N
Herrera	Chenci (51)	Single	Latinx	Lorenzo (27), Noah (15), *Naruto (12)*	Y-FT
Howard	Alice (70)	Extended kin— grandmother	Black	Daughter, *Eli (13), Malik (17), Tyler*	N
Jenkins	Diahann (74)	Extended kin— grandmother	Black	*Andre (18), Bryant (16)*	N*
Jimenez	Valentina (51)	Two parent— married	Latinx	*Amskan (16), Blanca (26), Amalia (14)*	Y-PT
Johnson	Sasha (39)	Single	Black	Nicholas (19), Tyrone (17), *Aaron (17), Brianna (5)*	Y-FT
Kiernan	Eartha (36)	Single	Biracial	*Jojo (14)*	Y-FT*
King	Jessica (45)	Extended kin— aunt	Black	Ashley (29), *Shannon (13), Bryson (16)*	Y-FT*

Family Last Name	Parents in Study (age)	Household Structure	Race/ Ethnicity of Parents	Children (ages) Italicized in Household	Currently Working FT: Full-Time PT: Part-Time (* if middle class)
Lee	Luz (52)	Two-parent— married	Latinx	*Marvin (20), Nolan (18)*	Y-FT (dad)*
Logan	Penny (41)	Single	White	*Shadow (14), Tori (7), Seth (5)*	N
Lopez	Leisy (50)	Single	Latinx	Fernando (35), Tommy (33), Javier (28), Kenny (22), Joel (23), Daisy (25), *Kobe (15)*	N
Lugo	Fernanda (47)	Single	Latinx	*Amanda (18), Max (12) Augustin (17)*	Y-FT
Martinez	Norma (35)	Single	Latinx	*Elisa (14), Isaac (11), Bruno (9)*	N
Medina	Maria (39)	Two-parent— married/stepdad	Latinx	*Gabriel (21), Carlos (15), David (10)*	N
Mitchell	Gabrielle (36)	Single	Black	*Cynthia (16), Jackie (18)*	N
Moore	Iesha (50)	Single	Black	Vanessa (29), Todd (27), *Alexa (17)*	N
Munoz	Cecelia (60)	Extended kin— grandparents	Latinx	Daughter, *Simon (15), Adrian, (14), Ian (12)*	N
Nelson	Elliott (57)	Single	Black	19 other children, *Matthew (15), Greg (12)*	N
Parker	Miranda (36)	Single	Black	*Brittany (21), Steven (14), 4 more children (17, 13, 10, 9)*	N
Pena	Eva (42)	Single	Latinx	*Matias (8), Felipe (13), Pablo (15)*	Y-PT

Family Last Name	Parents in Study (age)	Household Structure	Race/ Ethnicity of Parents	Children (ages) Italicized in Household	Currently Working FT: Full-Time PT: Part-Time (* if middle class)
Ramirez	Camila (40)	Two-parent— married/stepdad	Latinx	*Kelvin (21)*, *Tomas (16)*, 1 more child	Y-FT
Ramos	Nery (42)	Single	Latinx	Jariel (25), Rafael 22), Luis (20), *Abril (15)*	Y-FT
Reed	Leah (35)	Two-parent— married	White	*Charlie (15)*, *Nikki (11)*, Rob (18)	Y-FT (dad)
Reyes	Isadora (35)	Two-parent— married	Latinx	*Alvaro (12)*, *2 sons and 1 daughter (7, 4, 10)*	Y-FT
Roberts	Sarah (38)	Two-parent	Biracial	*Josh (16)*, *May (15)*	Y -FT (dad)
Romero	Angelica 35	Two-parent— married/stepdad	Latinx	*Layla (17)*, *Antonio (11)*, *Alma (15)*	Y-FT
Salazar	Juana (34)	Two-parent— married/stepdad	Latinx	*Leon (16)*	N
Scott	Angela (54)	Single	Black	*Jason (16)*, 9 brothers *(4 in household)*	Y-FT
Simmons	Renata (41)	Single	Black	*Omar (17)*, *Stacey (15)*, 2 more children	N
Smith	Believer 45	Single	White	*Gaby (12)*, *Lily (10)*, *Ivan (7)*	N
Soto	Julio (43)	Two-parent— married	Latinx	*Juliana (13)*, *Paola (7)*, *Carolina (7)*, *Elizabeth (8)*, *Leo (6)*, *Vicente (1)*	Y-PT
Strong	Iris (57)	Extended kin— grandparents	Latinx	Lola (35), 4 grandchildren, *Carmelo (15)*	N
Taylor	Sheree (48) & Randall (45)	Two-parent— married	Black	*Maya (14)*	Y-FT (dad)*

Family Last Name	Parents in Study (age)	Household Structure	Race/ Ethnicity of Parents	Children (ages) Italicized in Household	Currently Working FT: Full-Time PT: Part-Time (* if middle class)
Thomas	Talia (36) & Michael	Two-parent—stepdad	Biracial	*MJ (17)*, *Samuel (16)* *Aliyah (14)*, *Mia (5)*	N
Valdez	Carmin (35)	Single	Latinx	Valeria (14), Franco (11), *Jennifer (15)*	N
Velez	Lita & Juan (60)	Two-parent—married	Latinx	Rosie (35), *Albert (30)*, *Isabel (15)*, *Peter (11)*	Y-FT (dad)
Williams	Karen (36)	Single	Black	*Savannah (12)*, Keisha (19), *Ava (3)*	N
Wilson	Michelle (41)	Single	Black	*Shakera (14)*, *Kevin (2)*	Y-PT
Zapatero	Lena (51)	Single	Latinx	*Ignacio (13)*, *Joaquin (6)*	N

Notes

PROLOGUE

1. As a formatting note, I refer to the youth and parents by their full name the first time they appear in the chapter, so that readers can find them more easily in appendix B, and subsequently only by their first names. All names of people and organizations are pseudonyms.

2. While the staff's racial background was not noted here, this interaction might be seen as an instance of racial microaggression in that the medical staff member seems to doubt the Hernandezes, a poor family of color, and to discount my research assistant, Jerry. It is possible the man assumed Jerry was part of their family since he didn't ask him to clarify his relationship to them and they are from the same racial/ethnic background.

CHAPTER I. INTRODUCTION

1. Put another way, these institutions differ from ones that handle specific tasks (e.g., utilities, identifications, licensing, goods) in that the focus is on people and their needs, not objects to be consumed or sold. Yeheskel Hasenfeld depicts these types of institutions as "people processing institutions" (2009), or ones that are working to improve or change peoples' behaviors and lives. That goal then makes the outcomes of "success" harder to measure to some degree, versus clear-cut activities or tangible and clearly outlined outcomes such as profit margins, waiting times, or numbers of driver licenses issued per day.

2. To be clear, institutional mismatch is not to be confused with mismatch theory, which Richard Sander and Stuart Taylor Jr. (2012) use to critique affirmative action in law schools. The idea of institutional mismatch is to convey

the institutions' inability to respond to families' needs, versus focusing on the families' "deficiencies" in meeting institutional expectations. In using the term *institutional mismatch*, I also do not mean to suggest a fatalistic view that institutions should give up trying to work with families but rather, that we need to address the larger social, economic, and political context for those institutional limitations.

3. I worked with these agencies because my study initially was focused on family involvement in adolescent cases in social control institutions, comparing how that occurred in punitive organizations like the courts and therapeutic ones like the hospital. Yet what quickly became apparent was that the extent and substance of families' involvement in their youths' cases were not necessarily related to whether the institution was therapeutic (e.g., hospital overseeing a youth's asthma) or punitive (e.g., juvenile court addressing a youth's arrest) as much as it stemmed from the family's involvement across many institutions for that teenager and other family members. That is, the parents had to deal with several agencies for issues related to the entire household, themselves, and their children, which shaped how they negotiated the responsibilities for the initial focal institutions.

4. To clarify, some hospitals in this study are not technically public institutions. However I include them here for two reasons. One, they accept public insurance (Medicaid) which most of the families had. Two, the hospitals are similar to the other institutions in this study in that they are social control institutions. That is, they seek to modify the youth and parents' health behaviors according to what they believe to be medically appropriate. To do that, they do more than just try to encourage change; they often invoke (or threaten to invoke) the influence of other agencies such as child welfare to compel the parents to follow their recommendations.

5. These numbers are based on 162 children in the sixty-three households. If I included all children who may or may not be living in their households who were mentioned by the parents/legal guardians, the total number would increase to 245, the range of children per family would expand to one to twenty-one.

6. The age and gender range was based on 162 youths living in the sixty-three households; I do not know the age and gender of three youths from two households, the ages of two children in two other households, or the gender of two children in two additional households. If I included all 245 children, the gender ratios would be slightly different (58% males and 42% females) and the age range of the youths would be one to thirty-five years old. Again, to clarify, I do not know the gender for thirty-seven children (thirty-two of whom were living outside of the household) and do not have the ages of fifty-six youths (fifty-one of whom were living outside of the household).

7. I did not ask parents about their income, asking instead if they were working, either part-time or full-time, and in what capacity.

8. I should note that I did not get the work status for two of the families (3% of sample).

9. By scheduling issues, I refer both to the family and my respective schedules. For the majority of this project, I had to balance the fieldwork with my teaching responsibilities; families also had other pressing issues (e.g., taking a sick family member to the doctor, going to fix a problem with their food stamps

or their public assistance case) that led to them canceling our appointments. By communication issues, I refer to the families' occasional delays in responding to my attempts to contact them via phone, text, or mail; often it was due to the multiple issues going on in their lives. I describe the logistical challenges in doing this kind of fieldwork in appendix A.

10. On the view of institutions as a collective disciplinary force, see Soss, Fordham, and Schram (2011). Grubb and Lazerson (1982: 43) characterize instances where institutions both "help" and "keep order" as part of the "dual solution" regarding the state's responsibility for children: it justifies its intervention into family life only in instances where the family is in crisis or dysfunction but also crafts interventions (e.g., children's institutions) in ways that "sidestep the economic and social basis" for those situations. See also Foucault (1977, 1991) and Donzelot ([1979]1997).

11. See Garland (2016).

12. See Piven and Cloward (1971/1993) for a classic study about institutions "regulating the poor" as well as Fernandez-Kelly (2015).

13. See Lens (2012), and Handler (1986) for the blurring of systems and Luxton (2010) for the neoliberal focus on individual responsibility. See also Fong (2020: 610), who describes the "coupling of assistance with coercive authority" as the "hallmark of contemporary poverty governance."

14. Wacquant (2009), Soss et al. (2011), Quadagno (1994), and Garland (2001, 2016) all discuss the criminalization of poverty and its impact particularly on poor minority families. See also Haggerty and Ericson (2000, 2006) for more about surveillant assemblages, and Fong (2020) on the long-term punitive effects on families involved in the child welfare system who become "hypervisible" to and apprehensive of state institutions, even for those whose cases were unsubstantiated.

15. Blum writes,

Several [mothers] . . . were compelled to turn to the state and negotiate for meager public resources to care for vulnerable kids. But in a nation still clinging to a married-couple norm and demonizing public dependence, accessing benefits through Medicaid for health coverage, Section 8 for public housing and rent subsidies, the reformed welfare system from time-limited cash assistance, or the most convoluted, Supplemental Security Income for low-income families with disabled children, requires tremendous vigilant efforts and brings a degree of surveillance in exchange for paltry assistance—surveillance that was strikingly more intrusive and threatening for the single mothers and women of color. Ironically, however, state programs—when they worked—also offered genuinely helpful programs, particularly in child mental health services, services largely unavailable or difficult to obtain privately. (2015: 254)

16. Dewey and St. Germain (2016) do discuss the fragmented nature of the criminal justice and social service alliance in their book, talking about the variation among the organizations as well as the moments of discretion that individual staff exercise in working with the women. They also introduce the term *systemic intimacy* to capture the typically oppositional character to the interactions between the women and staff as shaped by their interpersonal dynamics, the cultural discourses about the women, and the systemic forces that shape the criminal justice–social service alliance's work. Despite the analytical nuance

provided by this concept, the authors still use it in line with their overall argument about the alliance's totalizing punitive effect on women.

17. Ray goes on to write, "Racialized organizations expand or inhibit agency, legitimate unequal distribution of resources, treat Whiteness as a credential, and decouple organizational procedures in ways that typically advantage dominant racial groups" (2019: 46).

18. See Bourdieu (1977).

19. Another related line of research in this area focuses on the ways that individual institutions affect families' lives. The welfare literature looks at the institutional policies shaping women's decisions about motherhood, marriage, and work; notions of independence and dependency; and issues of trust in their partners, bosses, and others (Edin and Lein 1997, Edin and Kefalas 2005, Hays 2003, Rodgers-Dillon and Haney 2005, Levine 2013, and Watkins-Hayes 2009). In the justice context, the collateral consequences of mass incarceration include barriers to employment (Pager 2007) and restrictions on family receipt of public benefits such as TANF, food stamps, and Medicaid, all of which negatively impact children's health and educational outcomes and parents' ability to pay child support (Sugie 2012; Wakefield and Wildeman 2013; Wildeman, Wakefield, and Lee 2016). Mass incarceration also leads people to engage in system avoidance (Goffman 2014 and Brayne 2014). For hospital settings, see Heimer and Staffen (1995, 1998); for child welfare settings, see Haney (2018), Reich (2005), and Waller (2019).

20. For example, Janet Shim (2010) uses the idea of "cultural health capital" to highlight parents' use of knowledge and resources specifically in the realm of health for their youth; Gengler (2014) and Gage-Bouchard (2017) build on that idea to show how parents invoke it while interacting with medical providers and also how those providers interpret those parental actions.

21. These institutional conundrums are in addition to the larger structural issues that we typically cite as challenges for poor families such as food deserts, insufficient housing, and low-paying jobs. The authors do deepen our understanding of those challenges with the families' stories. That is, food deserts, or the lack of groceries that have healthy food options in the neighborhood, lead poor families to spend more time, money, and effort than other families to seek out such options in other neighborhoods. Insufficient or lack of affordable housing means families must make do with overcrowded living conditions that physically do not have the space for families to eat together at one table or have the cooking equipment (e.g., knives, plates, stove) to prepare home-cooked meals. Finally, low-paying jobs with irregular work schedules make it hard to have a consistent time to eat dinner together as a family, given the unpredictable timing of those schedules taking away the families' control over its own time and wreaking havoc on the family's ability to ensure childcare.

22. In doing so, I prioritize families' accounts (Scott and Lyman 1968) for these involvements. As such, I am not focusing on the institutional accuracy of these families' claims but rather, how families understand and interact with the institutions.

23. For readability issues, I only mention a family's socioeconomic status if they are middle class. Otherwise, the family being discussed is poor.

24. Sharkey (2013) describes this phenomenon as "linked lives," in which the youths' life chances are inherently shaped by those of their parents and vice versa.

CHAPTER 2. CONCURRENT INVOLVEMENT

1. For examples of the policy discussions, see Herz et al. (2012) and Pennell, Shapiro, and Spigner (2011) on how to improve services between juvenile court and child welfare settings.

2. Suboxone is a combination of buprenorphine, which gives a mild effect of opioid use, and naloxone, which blocks the effects of opioids. It is used to manage opiate addiction, as it tricks the body into thinking it has taken the opioid while also preventing it from feeling any effects of opioids, should the person try to take it.

3. She is balancing all of these institutional involvements while also dealing with her extended family members' situations. Leisy's boyfriend, Carter, occasionally spends time with them in her apartment; he has institutional involvements related to his mental health and drug issues, for which she has to dedicate some time and energy. For example, Carter was arrested around the same time that Leisy was working on Kobe's SSI case and her other obligations; she helps his elderly and frail mother, who does not speak English, navigate that system, and she also visits him in jail. Meanwhile, her brother's twenty-seven-year-old son was shot and killed in a drug-related incident at a club, further adding grief to Leisy and her siblings, who lost their mother the year before, and also bringing up memories about her own past drug use. Finally, her younger sister is about to be evicted from their mother's apartment, which also reminds Leisy about her family's lack of support for her housing problems in the past.

4. It could be that the school called but couldn't leave a message on her phone. Her voicemail box is often full when I call her; she doesn't know how to retrieve or delete messages. I would have to call her repeatedly, and eventually, she would pick up on one of my calls. So, if the school relied primarily on phone calls to communicate with parents but did not call multiple times, that could explain why it took so long for her to find out.

5. Due to the timing of the notice of the absences and also Kobe's continuing medical issues, Leisy, the school, and ACS are not able to arrange a tutor for Kobe before the end of the school year. Kobe ends up going to summer school near his house; Leisy wants to switch him to a school closer to their house so she can make sure he is attending.

6. Poor families typically live in the outer boroughs of New York City, where public transportation typically takes longer than in or near Manhattan, where the subways and buses run more frequently and the distances are shorter.

7. It is not clear whether she could ask to refill the medication in advance. Typically these clinics operate under strict rules about the timing of refills to avoid patients potentially misusing the medication.

8. I'm not sure if the man was from the welfare office, but Leisy believes him to be from there.

9. Fernandez-Kelly (2015) also talks about former partners or children calling child welfare on the custodial parents.

10. Lita later tells me she has to move around a lot due to her bad back seizing up if she sits for too long.

11. While it has been eighteen months since Elena has been approved for Section 8 Housing, her apartment search is shaped by different institutional policies. It not only has to be eligible for Section 8, but also within a certain geographical area, as dictated by Family Court, because her ex, Lita's son, has an order of protection against her.

CHAPTER 3. REVISITING THE PAST

1. Talia mentions her mom was a sex worker and eventually was murdered by a serial killer. While I initially found the murder story a bit extreme, Talia showed me an article about her mom's death.

2. This program is the same one mentioned in the prologue that Gigi tried unsuccessfully to do.

3. It could be that she doesn't have the HPD paperwork or they haven't sent it to her yet. Regardless, that doesn't help her situation here.

4. I only have Melissa's account of events; I was unable to interview Evelyn because she was in a residential group home during the time I was doing these interviews with Melissa.

5. It is interesting to note that Marsha does not ask the court staff to clarify her questions about the paperwork but seeks out her own independent understanding at the library. So, it is not that she has an increased sense of trust in the court staff after her experience but rather that she believes that she needs to be an informed participant in the proceedings.

6. In a separate but related incident, Samuel's stepfather, Michael, took him to the hospital while he was in the middle of a fit; Talia said you could see it in his eyes that something is not right. However according to Talia, because Michael did not legally adopt Samuel, the hospital would not let him admit Samuel into the hospital. While it may not be the actual rules, Talia understood it to be the reason for what happened. Like Talia, several families reported similar kinds of situations where the mothers officially are still married to their exes while being in a relationship with new people, many of whom had a longer or closer bond with the children than the biological fathers. In these situations, institutions face the challenge in accommodating these families' situations when the stepparent is not officially listed on the records, if they are even aware of them.

7. On a related note, Lita's past experiences reveal another aspect of the temporal influence on current institutional involvement: the lasting emotional impact of one institutional involvement on a person. Her daughter died twenty years ago of cancer at ten years old. The impact of her daughter's death on Lita is evident, as she mentions it in every conversation and visit that I make to the home. Here is an excerpt from our first interview discussing how she manages her grief today:

> Lita: After my daughter passed away . . . I went there [a counseling center] because
> I went into depression and I still go through a lot of depression and a lot of anxious
> . . . but I know how to handle it now a little bit.

Leslie: When you were saying you know how to manage it a little bit, what do you do to manage?

Lita: I just go lock mysef in my room and I stay there. . . . I make believe I'm sleepy, so they don't bother me.

Lita's grief impacts how present and involved she is in her family's affairs, such as her fifteen-year-old adopted daughter Isabel's weight issues. Later in the interview when I ask if they ever disagree about how to handle Isabel's medical issues, she says, "We start arguing and we keep going on and I get frustrated and I say, 'You know what, leave it alone, go to your room, go watch TV, go—I don't know what you want to do. Go clean your room. Leave me alone. Go clean your room.'" Combined with the earlier comment about how she handles her grief, we see how her daughter's illness and death shape her disengagement from dealing with Isabel's chronic illness. However, it is not obvious to her family to see Lita's response as grief because Lita does not share with them why she needs to be alone. Instead, Lita's actions appear more as nagging Isabel about household chores, further distancing both her and the youth from addressing the medical issue at hand. In this case, Lita's past involvement dealing with a sick family member indirectly informs her approach now to her family, including their current institutional involvements such as Isabel's weight issues.

8. This perspective is reflective of what others (Gage-Bouchard 2017, Gengler 2014) have called a middle-class parental strategy of high involvement and active monitoring of a youth's condition, along with instructing the youth how to monitor it.

9. Janet Shim (2010) would see this action as part of a family's cultural health capital, referring to the knowledge, beliefs, and skills that families have to deal with a medical problem. See also Heritage and Robinson (2006), who discuss the idea of "doctorability," or how patients articulate their reasons for coming to the doctor as medically appropriate and legitimate.

10. See Gage-Bouchard (2017) for more on how cultural health capital needs to be studied not just in terms of patients' knowledge about their health but how they apply that knowledge in interactions with the doctors.

11. See Brandão, Lopes, and Ramos (2013).

12. As evidence of his concern, consider this prior conversation between Dr. Peters, Sulia, and Gigi that takes place when he interrupts an interview I was doing with them in his clinic's conference room. He reminds them to make an appointment with these words:

Dr. Peters: Your eyes, your kidneys, your long-term health are affected by this. And I don't want you living any shorter than you should be living. Right? I want you old. I want you watching *Golden Girls* reruns. I want you complaining about the weather. All that stuff. But all that gets affected by diabetes if you're not under control. . . . I'm really glad you came to me as a doctor. I'm really glad you came and agreed to do lab work. But once you were diagnosed, the idea is to do something about it. . . . So, what happens if you don't get what you need at a restaurant? You call the waitress over and you get what you want.

Gigi: No. No. I would call the manager if the waitress messes up.

Sulia: (laughs)

Dr. Peters: Exactly . . . that kind of initiative, you see what I'm saying here?

Gigi: Yeah.

Dr. Peters: Compare that to, "I'm just waiting for them to call." I need you to be that, that, that chick.

Gigi: Okay.

Dr. Peters: Where is the manager? Right? If you call and, "Can I speak to whoever manages the call center? Can I speak to a supervisor?"

Sulia: This is what I did. . . .

Dr. Peters: Right. Because what is, what's at stake here?

Sulia: They keep telling me they're going to call.

He is trying here to stress the importance of taking a proactive approach to Gigi's health. By first addressing Gigi, Dr. Peters appears to associate Sulia's waiting to make an appointment with her daughter not being assertive enough with her health. At the same time, even though Gigi says she knows to ask for help or to complain about the poor service in restaurants, her initiative is not relevant here, as she relies on Sulia to make her medical appointments. Moreover, Sulia says she does use those strategies of asking for a supervisor, but they do not appear to help, as the clinic staff members keep saying "they're going to call." Later, after Dr. Peters leaves, Sulia reiterates to me that the clinic keeps putting her on hold several times, even after she does call back. While both Sulia and Gigi state they know what to do and Sulia tells me that she has done what Dr. Peter suggests, neither Dr. Peters nor the institution appear to validate their efforts "to do something about it."

13. According to WebMD, the target number for people with diabetes should be less than 7. https://www.webmd.com/diabetes/guide/glycated-hemoglobin-test-hba1c.

14. See also Jacobs (1990).

CHAPTER 4. WHO'S IN THE FAMILY?

1. To some degree, previous research has recognized how this fluidity might affect poor families. Demographers (Mare 2015; McLanahan 2009) acknowledge and incorporate changing family patterns such as blended households, extended kin guardianship, single parenthood, and multi-partner fertility in studies of household influences on individuals' social mobility. Qualitative research has found strengths in families relying on extended kin (Stack 1974) or opportunities through the disposable ties within the family's social network (Desmond 2012; Mazelis 2017) to mitigate the conditions of poverty; at the same time, those same types of supports weaken the communities in general, as limited resources are shared among more people. While these studies recognize the limitations of traditional definitions of family households (e.g., nuclear family versus single parents) in studying intergenerational poverty, the meaning of extended family ties or broader social networks as it pertains to institutional involvements has not been sufficiently explored. Poor families might rely on

disposable ties to address immediate material needs. However, they might be less likely to use those ties to manage institutional obligations, especially considering many institutions effectively operate with fixed notions of households or with limitations of who is able to be involved in such cases.

2. See also Paik (2011, 2017).

3. It takes at least an hour from Eileen's house by public bus to get to the ferry in Staten Island; the ferry leaves between two to three times an hour during the day to Manhattan. It also takes an hour by bus to get to the nearest subway station in Brooklyn. Express buses into Manhattan take less time but cost more than double what the regular bus, ferry, and subway cost ($6.00 one way, compared to $2.50 in 2013 when I was doing fieldwork with this family).

4. For example, a thirteen-year-old Black youth, Edward Bryant, was in juvenile court for a less serious charge of theft. However, he stayed in the same neighborhood and became "known" to the local police as someone to keep under supervision, getting rearrested constantly for probation violations. Edward ended up in a long-term group home.

5. Eileen explained to me that she tried to file for divorce three times, but Phil never signed the papers. He now says he will sign if she draws up the papers again. However, Eileen wants him to initiate the process because for her to do so, she'd have to go through welfare (which she did the other three times) because she cannot afford to pay the filing fees herself. She didn't want to deal with that hassle again.

6. Eileen says Phil gives her $80 a month in child support for Brian. But Phil is not consistent in when he gives Brian any spending money.

7. John mentions to me separately that he receives a pension from this job but wants to find another job to make some extra money.

8. In line with the theme of concurrent involvements discussed in the previous chapter, Eileen has difficulties in getting therapy for Patrick. Many of the providers, including one that saw him previously, will not accept him because of his current probation status. So one institutional involvement (e.g., juvenile court) then could affect her compliance in another institution (e.g., child welfare). She ends up finding a program, not disclosing up front that it is a probation-mandated appointment. When she did tell the counselor that Patrick is on probation during the intake, the counselor said the other programs are not allowed to reject clients based on their probation status.

9. I should note that I never talked to the child welfare workers or to Patrick about this issue. This example is based on what I gleaned from Eileen in our conversation and then verified by the court diversion staff a few months later.

10. Eileen tells me that FEGS is for people on welfare who don't work. She has to go to welfare to get recertified and to FEGS to ask for services like Brian's camp and childcare provider or to drop off the papers regarding her not being able to work. According to its website, FEGS was a nonprofit and filed for bankruptcy in 2015.

11. Isabel told me they only use that bathroom because it has a full shower and toilet. I once did go into the second bathroom and saw what looked like bedpans for the uncle.

12. I should note that Albert and Amanda also help take care of Lita's bed-ridden brother, in whose name the apartment lease is, when the others are not at home. So perhaps Lita also sees the benefits to having them stay in the house.

13. She is referring to the Metformin that Isabel is supposed to take for her weight issues.

14. It is unclear why they didn't transfer the case immediately to another diversion agency in Brooklyn. His probation supervision was eventually transferred to Brooklyn.

15. Shakera was sixteen years old when this conversation occurred.

CHAPTER 5. MITIGATING FACTORS

1. As stated in the introduction, *institutional mismatch* is not to be conflated with Sander and Taylor's mismatch theory about affirmative action (2012). My intent is to highlight the institutional inability to (1) address the complexity of familys' issues and (2) recognize its part in contributing to the families' continued or escalating involvements across institutions.

2. Of particular relevance for the Bryants' journey in the maze, that past experience of getting evicted from public housing—beyond giving her night-mares—informs how Catherine approaches her relationship with her landlord now. She recently overpaid her rent by $800 one month without questioning it (her rent typically was $212) because she didn't want to endanger her housing situation. Here's how she described the situation to me during a home visit:

> Her rent went up by $800. She paid it but didn't understand why it went up so much. . . . She said that she doesn't mess with the rent because she doesn't want to get kicked out of her home. It turns out that she should have only had to pay $400 or something like that; she is working with the landlord to figure out the payment plan.

3. This placement appears to be another instance of institutional mismatch based on what is written on his IEP (individualized education plan), which Catherine showed me in a previous visit:

> He is listed as average in functioning, verbal/math, excellent in memory and below average in "processing" (which I think meant perceptual reasoning). She reads through it and points out that he separates from kids when needed and that he doesn't pay attention sometimes. I also remember reading he is restless and talks with other students while the teacher is talking. At the same time, the report said that he did pay attention after the teacher called him out on it and also helped her clean up after the lesson. Catherine said his teachers at school tell her how good a student he is and that he is smart. Catherine says she always knew that he just needs to behave better sometimes.

As Edward is not designated as needing special education in the IEP, it is not clear whether or not this home is the right fit for him. The home does try to get him a job through the city's summer youth employment program. But paperwork issues delay that process, as Catherine has to provide his birth certificate and social security number, the latter of which needs to be given twice because the social worker there asked for it again. Edward eventually ran away from the facility and was arrested for robbery. He was then sent to a more secure facility upstate.

4. In contrast, consider Patrick Fouskas, a white thirteen-year-old, from chapter 4. He was on probation for arson and also had ADHD, like Edward. However, he managed to stay "compliant" with probation, even though he was not on medication and spent months being truant from school.

5. Moreover, the hospital would not admit Samuel for an emergency hold because his stepfather took him and apparently did not have the legal right to do so. Both institutions—the court and hospital—did not get Samuel on the right treatment path, which complicated his court case and the family's other institutional involvements. That case shows how families can get caught in the web of interagency issues and conflicts that prevent them from getting the suitable help for mental illness.

6. One could envision that interaction going in different ways depending on the officers and extent of mental health training they might have. See Emerson and Pollner (2019) for more on the organizational contingencies and issues affecting the response of combined police-psychiatric response teams. More often than not, police are not trained in mental health issues, leading them to misinterpret a mentally ill person's actions as threatening, particularly if it is a person of color, or to not know how to diffuse mounting tensions in these situations.

7. While not addressed in this chapter, mental health issues also reveal the flaws in organizations' policies, which often require a clear-headed focus to parse through the various requirements. For example, as discussed in chapter 2, Leisy Lopez had difficulties in trying to figure out the paperwork deadlines for her son's SSI case, partly due to her confusion that results as a side effect of her mental health medications.

8. Catherine mentions that point to me during a home visit.

9. It is unclear whether Edward's lawyer or Sarah knew of the alleged abuse by Edward toward Rodney. I would imagine that if they had known, they would not have advocated for him to return to a house shared by a potential victim of his alleged sexual abuse.

10. Kevin's father is not Kwame, her daughter's father, who is mentioned in the last chapter.

11. Referring back to Patrick Fouskas's court case from the previous chapter, the multihousehold factor allowed for his potential abuse to slip through the cracks, as the diversion agency in Staten Island (where the court case started) did not have enough time to work with him to assess the seriousness of the situation with his father, with whom he lived in Brooklyn. So while his alleged abuse could have been equally untreated like Micah and Edward, it did not affect his court case, for which he was given more leniency by probation, most likely due to his racial privilege.

12. To clarify, I did not ask families in the interviews about their legal status in the country. While it would have been helpful to know how that status affected their institutional involvement, it did not feel appropriate for the onetime interviews to do so. Also, in New York City, families, regardless of immigrant status, could still access services such as Medicaid (emergency and

prenatal care, health care for children under nineteen) or benefits for family members who are citizens. I did ask the two immigrant families in the ethnography, the Cabreras and the Wilsons, only after I felt that I had built up sufficient rapport and trust with them to ask if they voluntarily would share. In those cases, both families had legal status with one becoming naturalized citizens.

13. Consider this fieldnote excerpt from a court hearing where the judge is deciding whether to place Richard in a twelve-month drug treatment program.

> [Before the hearing] Sofia says she is nervous and this is "too much." . . . She said Richard told her that he is not an addict so why should he go away for that? She adds he only smoked marijuana one time, not cocaine or heroin. . . . We wait almost an hour to go into the courtroom. The court officer brings us into the room right before the courtroom. Sofia seems to get more nervous now as she looks into the window of the door to see who is in there. She says "please, God" a couple times and sighs a few times more. . . . The court officer says they are waiting for the Spanish interpreter. Sofia says it's ok to start without the interpreter, but the court officer says he already called for one. She said again it was ok; the court officer says he will ask the judge. Before he can get a response [from the judge], the interpreter arrives.
>
> The judge says we are on for disposition and that MHS [mental health agency] submitted a report . . . that recommends non-secure detention where Richard can get mental health treatment, substance abuse treatment, and school. The judge then asks the probation officer what he recommends. The probation officer says they need time to fax out that MHS report to suitable programs. The judge says they will adjourn [for two weeks later to give probation that time]. He then asks Sofia if that is ok and she says yes without waiting for the interpreter to say anything. . . . The judge doesn't ask Sofia any other questions or ask if she understands what's going on. I notice that she says something to the interpreter who doesn't respond, nor communicate to the judge or lawyer what Sofia said. . . . The whole process takes less than 5 minutes. After Richard and Sofia leave, the judge asks the probation officer if Richard's other siblings were also in the system, saying "aren't all three kids not so desirable?" or something like that. . . . After a few minutes, the judge appears to have read Richard's file and confirms that all three were in the system.

Sofia's anxiety here is front and center, only getting heightened by the hour-long wait for the hearing to start. Even though there is an interpreter present to convey Sofia's initial concerns about Richard going to a drug treatment program, she does not raise her objections to or questions about the necessity of drug treatment. But given the judge's comment, "Aren't all three kids not so desirable?" it is not clear if the judge would have been swayed by her input when he considered the sons' past history in the court.

14. See also Leslie Reese (2001) who uses Suarez-Orozco's notion of a "dual frame of reference" (1989) to describe this phenomenon of immigrant adults comparing their experiences in the United States to their situation in their home country, including their understanding of institutions. For a more recent discussion on how immigrant families fare in the United States, see Rendon (2019) who focuses on the structural and neighborhood level factors shaping those families' lives in more complicated ways, versus simply attributing the youths' outcomes to segmented assimilation (Portes and Rumbaut 2001).

15. See Goffman's "Insanity of Place" (1969) for a more general theoretical framework to capture this phenomenon of families seeking out help from

people or agencies outside of the home (what he refers to as "external econo-mies") only when they can no longer handle what they perceive to be prob-lems to their own way of structuring their household and relational dynamics ("internal economies").

16. Beyond the logistic and financial hardship in traveling back to Mexico to get these documents if they are available, Gabriela might also have to get them translated from Spanish into English to be accepted by the hospital.

CHAPTER 6. CONCLUSION

1. For example, think back to the child welfare agency's handling of Cath-erine Bryant's family over generations. Edward and Rodney both were exposed to abuse (Edward—physical, and Rodney—sexual), yet neither received coun-seling or treatment for it. While the long-term impact on them remains to be seen, Edward, both a victim of his father's abuse and alleged abuser to Rodney, already had extensive involvement in the juvenile justice system, disrupting his education and delaying his mental health treatment.

2. See Cottam (2018) who cites a public report from 2014 on government expenditures for "chaotic families" in the range of £250,000 per family, or $392,500, with no measurable success with reducing that involvement with families.

3. See Edin and Kafalas (2005).

4. See Schwartz (2013) for more on the way that the marriage market per-petuates and exacerbates social inequalities.

5. Hilary Cottam makes this point so eloquently when she writes,

> The welfare state . . . has become a management state: an elaborate and expensive sys-tem of managing needs and their accompanying risks. Those of us who need care, who can't find work, who are sick or less able are moved around as if in a game of pass-the-parcel: assessed, referred and then assessed again. Everyone suffers in a system where 80 per cent of the resource available must be spent on gate-keeping: on managing the queue, on referring individuals from service to service, on recording every interaction to ensure that no one is responsible for those who inevitably fall through the gaps. . . . Both [political] sides want to focus on the money and to rearrange the institutions. Above all, they want to manage things differently. But management is not going to work. In fact, it might make things worse. The more we concentrate on merely rework-ing our existing institutions, the more we fail to see or understand the nature of the new challenges that surround us. (2018: 190–202, 202–14)

6. Using an older example, COMPSTAT led to a change in policing, whereby arrest data was used to determine the shifting allocation of officers to patrol certain "hotspot" areas. Yet that only served to reinforce the ideas about "high crime" neighborhoods, versus a critical assessment of racialized police practices shaping officers' interactions with citizens in those neighborhoods.

7. As Herd and Moynihan (2018) suggest, we should be highly selective and critical in discerning whether technologies can facilitate case processing (e.g., DMV appointments, renewal of licenses) or impose greater harm in cases of error (e.g., denying health care to eligible children). Their words highlight

the conflicting ways that new technologies in governance are used. On the one hand, these technologies and automation could facilitate the cross-institutional sharing of information that reduces individuals' burdens to provide the same information repeatedly (O'Hara, Shattuck, and Goerge 2017); they could also identify additional resources for an individual if the same information is being evaluated by many different agencies and, if possible, might be used to auto-enroll them in those services. On the other hand, technology is not the magic solution for all situations, given the possibility of added surveillance of individuals (Brayne 2014). In addition, technology can exacerbate existing social inequalities, such as facial recognition tools that disproportionately misidentify people of color, particularly Blacks.

8. See their three tables (Herd and Moynihan 2018: 258, 259, 263) for detailed and informative diagnostic tools and techniques to reduce administrative burdens, as broken down by the learning, compliance, and psychological costs to individuals.

9. They (2018) also note that whether administrative burdens were intentional to the initial design or not, they could become part of the way to continually assess an institution's work, or a "new professional norm" to consider that work. If the burdens prove to be too much, especially in the sense of affecting certain groups disproportionately and in ways that exceed the intended positive effects of the institution, we could find different ways to shift the burden to the institution itself, instead of the individual. For more on carefully considering how to evaluate programs as they work on the ground, see Banerjee and Duflo (2011).

10. They recommend an equivalent of the GI Bill for "veterans" of disruptions, recognizing that investing in peoples' economic futures—whether via education or other social supports—in times of need is a better use of governmental time and resources than policing peoples' behaviors and curtailing their benefits if they prove "undeserving."

11. For more on Medicare for All, see Moffitt and Ziliak (2019) and Chandra and Garthwaite (2019). For more on Universal Basic Income, see Dynan's summary (2019) of Hoynes and Rothstein (2019).

12. The political and macroeconomic context obviously are both central to any policy reform. Herd and Moynihan talk about the political use of administrative burdens to further one's goal. While both conservative and liberal politicians could do so, the conservatives have developed a particular political use of burdens in two ways—one, as evidence of a program's "failure" (e.g., instances of fraud or red tape as "proving" an institution's inefficiency) and two, as a way to limit people's access to resources (e.g., increasing eligibility requirements to cut welfare rolls or more regulation to limit abortion) to cut back on programs or to further stigmatize the group affected by the policy. Another approach to consider politics and policy is how Hacker and Pierson discuss a policy's "positive political effects." They write (2019: 9): "Will this policy create positive political effects—that is, will it encourage ongoing and, ideally, increasing efforts to address the problem?"

Macroeconomic forces also are important to consider in any attempt to improve the efficacy of social safety net institutions. Those would include "rising government debt, slower macroeconomic growth, limited tools to fight future recessions, greater income inequality, and the financial struggles of many U.S. households" (Dynan 2019: 352). In that light, workfare programs should be designed and evaluated on more than just increasing labor participation among its participants; in addition to depending on the availability of such jobs for people to get, the "adequacy" of income derived from those jobs needs to be evaluated alongside the costs of that work (e.g., added childcare, transportation expenses) and the current state of our economy that features nontraditional work hours.

13. Lipsky (1980/2010) mentions a similar type of reinvestment in training for child welfare in his concluding chapter. As for which government agency should sponsor that training, I could see Health and Human Services—in collaboration with nonprofit family services organizations—as a possible option.

14. See Lemert (1967, 1981) and Schur (1973).

15. See Herd and Moynihan (2018) about "take up rates" that might be affected by the negative psychological costs of being stigmatized in these programs. Procedural justice (Tyler 2006) also is concerned with this idea of fairness in one interaction shaping people's views about and compliance with that institution and others.

16. They write (2018: 266): "Just as diagnosing a disease is not an attack on the patient, identifying burdens is not an attack on government. Rather, the diagnosis allows us to distinguish between burdens that are necessary or unnecessary and to understand that shifting burdens away from citizens requires administrative capacity. It offers us a framework to improve governance."

17. According to Cottam, this requires a more flexible approach where staff members from different organizations work with the families, coming up with creative solutions as informed by their expertise and training but not necessarily being bound to the rules of their respective organizations' protocols. In the US context, there are some current examples of this multi-team approach such as the IEP (individualized education plan) process for schools, which includes case conferences with families. But families are not necessarily equal contributors to the process.

18. See Maestas (2019) for more on this idea of partial disability benefits.

19. See Moffitt and Ziliak (2019) and Rachidi and Doar (2019).

POSTSCRIPT

1. I am only including updates on five of those families here, as the sixth was not featured in the book because the main components to its multi-institutional experiences were reflected in the other five families' stories that were presented here.

APPENDIX A

1. Eight other families signed up for the ethnography. While I did some more interviews with two families, I was not able to reach any of them to do all the follow-up interviews and visits over a twelve-month period. I did not officially

drop them from the study but stopped making attempts to contact them after several tries.

2. I use 2017, as that is the last year I conducted fieldwork.

3. I do not include ACS statistics on family structure because they are not comparable for two reasons: (1) they are defining two-parent families to only include married spouses and (2) the percentage breakdown in the ACS is based on all people living in poverty, including those without children

4. This percentage is for Hispanic or Latino origin of any race.

5. The NYC.gov measure is similar to the supplemental poverty measure for families with children under eighteen, which includes broader definitions of income and expenses, adjusted for the higher cost of living in New York City. The ACS uses the official poverty measure, which is based on stricter definition of income and food expenditures with no adjustment for geographic variations to cost of living. For more details on these measures, please see Chatterjee et al. (2019).

6. I use this timeframe as it was when I conducted interviews with the families whose youths had juvenile court cases. I should note that while the arrests declined each year (12,371 in 2011, 9,675 in 2012 and 7,604 in 2013), the racial breakdown remained largely the same. See Citizens' Committee for Youth of New York, Juvenile Arrests (Under 16 years) 2017, https://data.cccnewyork .org/data/map/46/juvenile-arrests-under-16-years#46/a/2/83/25/a.

7. See also Thorpe et al. (2004) for racial disparity in childhood obesity rates among New York City (NYC) elementary public school children. Regarding older youths, the NYC Department of Health and Mental Hygiene found in its Youth Risk Behavior Survey, an anonymous survey of public high school youth, that 12 percent of public high school students are obese and another 16 percent are overweight in 2015; in the same survey, 24 percent of high school youth in 2015 reported having asthma at some point in their lives, with 14 percent having an asthma attack in the last year.

8. Consider the statistics of poor families' involvement in other public institutions included in this study: according to the American Community Survey, almost one in five families in 2017 in New York City had food stamps in the last twelve months (19.8%), 7.6 percent received Supplemental Security Income, and 4.6 percent received public assistance. In addition, the rates of investigations for child welfare (abuse and neglect) are highest in the neighborhoods where my families lived; Citizens' Committee for Children's "Child Abuse and Neglect Investigations" analyzed data from Administration of Children Services' 2017 annual report and found indication rates in a range of 33–45 percent or an investigation rate of sixteen to sixty-five per one thousand children.

9. I chose not to reach out to the other fifty-three families who participated in the one-time interviews for two reasons. One, those interviews focused more on the youth's court or health-related case versus multi-institutional involvement specifically. Two, too much time had passed between the time I did those interviews and finished the analysis; I did not expect to be successful in trying to reach them.

10. This is akin to what Duneier describes as "checking stuff" in *Sidewalk* (1999).

References

Abraham, Laura Kaye. 2019/1993. *Mama Might Be Better Off Dead: The Failure of Health Care in Urban America*. 2nd edition. Chicago: University of Chicago Press.

Banerjee, Abhijit, and Esther Duflo. 2011. *Poor Economics: A Radical Rethinking of the Way to Fight Global Poverty*. New York: Public Affairs. Kindle.

Blum, Linda. 2015. *Raising Generation RX: Mothering Kids with Invisible Disabilities in an Age of Inequality*. New York: New York University Press.

Bourdieu, Pierre. 1977. "Cultural Reproduction and Social Reproduction." In *Power and Ideology in Education*, edited by J. Karabel and A. H. Halsey, 487–511. New York: Oxford University Press.

Bowen, Sarah, Joslyn Brenton, and Sinikka Elliott. 2019. *Pressure Cooker: Why Home Cooking Won't Solve Our Problems and What We Can Do about It*. New York: Oxford University Press. Kindle Edition.

Brandão, Mariana, Carla Lopes, and Elisabete Ramos. 2013. "Identifying Adolescents with High Fasting Glucose: The Importance of Adding Grandparents' Data When Assessing Family History of Diabetes." *Preventive Medicine* 57: 500–504.

Brayne, Sarah. 2014. "Surveillance and System Avoidance: Criminal Justice Contact and Institutional Attachment." *American Sociological Review* 79(3): 367–91.

Chandra, Amitabh, and Craig Garthwaite. 2019. "Economic Principles for Medicare Reform." *Annals of the American Academy of Political and Social Science* 686: 63–92.

Chatterjee, Debipriya, John Krampner, Jihyun Shin, Vicky Virgin, Yaoqi Li, Martha Moreno Perez, and Ningrui Zhang. 2019. *New York City Government Poverty Measure 2017: An Annual Report from the Office of the Mayor*. New York: NYC Mayor's Office for Economic Opportunity.

Citizens' Committee for Youth of New York. 2017a. Child Abuse and Neglect Investigations. https://data.cccnewyork.org/data/map/3/child-abuse-and-neglect-investigations#3/a/3/5/40/a.

———. 2017b. Juvenile Arrests (Under 16 Years) 2017. Accessed at https://data.cccnewyork.org/data/map/46/juvenile-arrests-under-16-years#46/a/2/83/25/a.

Cottam, Hillary. 2018. *Radical Help: How We Can Remake the Relationships between Us and Revolutionise the Welfare State.* New York: Virago. Kindle Edition.

Day, S. E., K. J. Konty, M. Leventer-Roberts, C. Nonas, and T. G. Harris. 2014. "Severe Obesity among Children in New York City Public Elementary and Middle Schools, School Years 2006–07 through 2010–11." Preventing Chronic Disease. 11:130439. DOI: http://dx.doi.org/10.5888/pcd11.130439.

Desmond, Matthew. 2012. "Disposable Ties and the Urban Poor." *American Journal of Sociology* 117(5): 1295–335.

Dewey, Susan, and Tonia St. Germain. 2016. *Women of the Street: How the Criminal Justice–Social Services Alliance Fails Women in Prostitution.* Kindle Edition. New York: New York University Press.

Donzelot, Jacques. 1979/1997. *The Policing of Families.* Translated by Robert Hurley. Baltimore: Johns Hopkins University Press.

Duflo, Esther, and Abhijit Banerjee. 2019 "Economic Incentives Don't Always Do What We Want Them to." Opinion, *New York Times*, October 26.

Duneier, Mitchell. 1999. *Sidewalk.* New York: Farrar, Straus and Giroux.

Dynan, Karen. 2019. "The Economic Context for Reforming the Safety Net." *Annals of the American Academy of Political and Social Science* 686: 352–68.

Edin, Kathryn, and Maria Kefalas. 2005. *Promises I Can Keep: Why Poor Women Put Motherhood before Marriage.* Berkeley: University of California Press.

Edin, Kathryn, and Laura Lein. 1997. *Making Ends Meet: How Single Mothers Survive Welfare and Low-Wage Work.* New York: Russell Sage Foundation.

Emerson, Robert, Rachel Fretz, and Linda Shaw. 2011. *Writing Ethnographic Fieldnotes.* 2nd edition. Chicago: University of Chicago Press.

Emerson, Robert M., and Melvin Pollner. 2019. "Contingent Control and Wild Moments: Conducting Psychiatric Evaluations in the Home." *Social Inclusion* 7(1): 259–68.

Fernandez-Kelly, Patricia. 2015. *The Hero's Fight: African Americans in West Baltimore and the Shadow of the State.* Princeton, NJ: Princeton University Press.

Fong, Kelley. 2020. "Getting Eyes in the Home: Child Protective Services Investigations and State Surveillance of Family Life." *American Sociological Review* 85(4): 610–38.

Foucault, Michel. 1977. *Discipline and Punish: The Birth of the Prison.* New York: Pantheon.

———. 1991. "Governmentality." In *The Foucault Effect: Studies in Governmentality*, edited by G. Burchell, C. Gordon, and P. Miller, 87–104. Chicago: University of Chicago Press.

Gage-Bouchard, Elizabeth. 2017. "Culture, Styles of Institutional Interactions, and Inequalities in Healthcare Experiences." *Journal of Health and Social Behavior* 58 (2): 147–65.

Garland, David. 2001. *The Culture of Control: Crime and Social Order in Contemporary Society*. Chicago: University of Chicago Press.

———. 2016. *Welfare State: A Very Short Introduction*. Oxford: Oxford University Press.

Gengler, Amanda. 2014. "I Want You to Save My Kid!": Illness Management Strategies, Access, and Inequality at an Elite University Research Hospital." *Journal of Health and Social Behavior* 55(3): 342–59.

Goffman, Alice. 2014. *On the Run: Fugitive Life in an American City*. Chicago: University of Chicago Press.

Goffman, Erving. 1969. "The Insanity of Place." *Psychiatry: Journal of Interpersonal Relations* 32: 357–87.

Grubb, W. Norton, and Marvin Lazerson. 1982. *Broken Promises: How Americans Fail Their Children*. New York: Basic Books.

Hacker, Jacob, and Paul Pierson. 2019. "Policy Feedback in the Age of Polarization." *Annals of the American Academy of Political and Social Science* 686: 8–28.

Haggerty, Kevin D., and Richard V. Ericson. 2000. "The Surveillant Assemblage." *British Journal of Sociology* 51:605–22.

———. 2006. *The New Politics of Surveillance and Visibility*. Toronto: University of Toronto Press.

Halpern-Meekin, Sarah. 2019. *Social Poverty: Low-Income Parents and the Struggle for Family and Community Ties*. New York: New York University Press.

Handler, Joel F. 1986. *The Conditions of Discretion: Autonomy, Community, Bureaucracy*. New York: Sage.

Haney, Lynne. 2018. "Incarcerated Fatherhood: The Entanglements of Child Support Debt and Mass Imprisonment." *American Journal of Sociology* 124(1): 1–48.

Hartman, Ann. (1995). "Diagrammatic Assessment of Family Relationships." *Families in Society* 76: 111–22.

Hasenfeld, Yeheskel. 2009. *Human Service as Complex Organizations*. 2nd edition. Thousand Oaks, CA: Sage.

Hays, Sharon. 2003. *Flat Broke with Children: Women in the Age of Welfare Reform*. New York: Oxford University Press.

Heimer, Carol, and Lisa Staffen. 1995. "Interdependence and Reintegrative Social Control: Labeling and Reforming 'Inappropriate' Parents in Neonatal Intensive Care Units." *American Sociological Review* 60: 635–54.

———. 1998. *For the Sake of the Children: The Social Organization of Responsibility in the Hospital and the Home*. Chicago: University of Chicago Press.

Herd, Pamela, and Donald P. Moynihan. 2018. *Administrative Burden: Policymaking by Other Means*. New York: Russell Sage Foundation.

Heritage, J., and J. Robinson. 2006. "Accounting for the Visit: Giving Reasons for Seeking Medical Care." In *Communication in Medical Care: Interactions between Primary Care Physicians and Patients*, edited by J. Heritage and D. W. Maynard. Cambridge: Cambridge University Press.

Herz, Denise, Philip Lee, Lorrie Lutz, Macon Stewart, John Tuell, and Janet Wiig. 2012. *Addressing the Needs of Multi-System Youth: Strengthening the Connection between Child Welfare and Juvenile Justice*. Washington DC: Center for Juvenile Justice Reform, Georgetown University.

Hoynes, Hilary, and Jesse Rothstein. 2019. "Universal Basic Income in the U.S. and Advanced Countries." *Annual Review of Economics* 11: 929–58.

Jacobs, Mark. 1990. *Screwing the System and Making It Work*. Chicago: University of Chicago Press.

Kohler-Hausmann, Issa. 2018. *Misdemeanorland: Criminal Courts and Social Control in an Age of Broken Windows Policing*. Princeton, NJ: Princeton University Press.

Lareau, Annette. 2003/2011. *Unequal Childhoods: Class Race, and Family Life* 2nd edition. Berkeley: University of California Press.

Lemert, Edwin. 1967. "The Juvenile Court—Quest and Realities." In *Task Force Report: Juvenile Delinquency and Youth Crime*. By President's Commission of Law Enforcement and Administration of Justice, 91–106. Washington, DC: Government Printing Office.

———. 1981. Diversion in Juvenile Justice: What Hath Been Wrought." *Journal of Research in Crime and Delinquency* 18(1): 34–46.

Lens, Vicki. 2012. "Judge or Bureaucrat? How Administrative Law Judges Exercise Discretion in Welfare Bureaucracies." *Social Science Review* 86(2): 269–93.

Levine, Judith. 2013. *Ain't No Trust: How Bosses, Boyfriends, and Bureaucrats Fail Low-Income Mothers and Why It Matters*. Berkeley: University of California Press.

Lipsky, Michael. 2010/1980. *Street-Level Bureaucracy: Dilemmas of the Individual in Public Services*. Updated edition. New York: Russell Sage Foundation.

Luxton, Meg. 2010. "Doing Neoliberalism in Everyday Personal Life." In *Neoliberalism and Everyday Life*, edited by Susan Braedley and Meg Luxton, 163–83. Montreal: McGill-Queens' University Press.

Maestas, Nicole. 2019. "Identifying Work Capacity and Promoting Work: A Strategy for Modernizing the SSDI Program." *Annals of the American Academy of Political and Social Science* 686: 93–120.

Mare, Robert. 2015. "Measuring Networks beyond the Origin Family." *The Annals of American Academy of Political and Social Science* 657: 97–107

Martinson, Robert. 1974. "What Works? Questions and Answers about Prison Reform." *The Public Interest* 35: 22–54.

Mazelis, Joan Maya. 2017. *Surviving Poverty: Creating Sustainable Ties among the Poor*. New York: New York University Press.

McLanahan, Sara. 2009. "Fragile Families and the Reproduction of Poverty." *The Annals of American Academy of Political and Social Science* 621: 111–31.

Moffitt, Robert A., and James P. Ziliak. 2019. "Entitlements: Options for Reforming the Social Safety Net in the United States." *Annals of the American Academy of Political and Social Science* 686: 8–35.

New York City Data Tool: Race and Ethnicity of Families with Children under 18. https://www1.nyc.gov/site/opportunity/poverty-in-nyc/data-tool.page.

New York City Department of Health and Mental Hygiene. Youth Risk Behavior Survey. https://a816-health.nyc.gov/hdi/epiquery/visualizations?PageType=ps&PopulationSource=YRBS.

O'Hara, Amy, Rachel M. Shattuck, and Robert M. Goerge. 2017. "Linking Federal Surveys with Administrative Data to Improve Research on Families." *Annals of the American Academy of Political and Social Sciences* 669: 63–74.

Pager, Devah. 2007. *Marked: Race, Crime, and Finding Work in an Era of Mass Incarceration*. Chicago: University of Chicago Press.

Paik, Leslie. 2011. *Discretionary Justice: Looking Inside a Juvenile Drug Court*. New Brunswick, NJ: Rutgers University Press.

———. 2017. "Rethinking Family Involvement in Juvenile Justice." *Theoretical Criminology* 21(3): 307–23.

Paik, Leslie, and Chiara Packard. 2019. "Impact of Juvenile Justice Fines and Fees on Family Life: Case Study in Dane County, WI." Philadelphia, PA: Juvenile Law Center.

Pennell, Joan, Carol Shapiro, and Carol Spigner. 2011. *Safety, Fairness, Stability: Repositioning Juvenile Justice and Child Welfare to Engage Families and Communities*. Washington DC: Center for Juvenile Justice Reform, Georgetown University.

Picard, Sarah, Matt Watkins, Michael Rempel, and Ashmini Kerodal. 2019. "Beyond the Algorithm: Pretrial Reform, Risk Assessment, and Racial Fairness." Center for Court Innovation. Accessed online at https://www.courtinnovation.org/publications/beyond-algorithm.

Piven, Francis Fox, and Richard Cloward. 1971/1993. *Regulating the Poor: The Functions of Public Welfare*. New York: Random House.

Portes, Alejandro, and Rumbaut, Ruben. 2001. *Legacies: The Story of the Immigrant Second Generation*. Berkeley: University of California Press.

Quadagno, Jill. 1994. *The Color of Welfare: How Racism Undermined the War on Poverty*. New York: Oxford University Press.

Rachidi, Angela, and Robert Doar. 2019. "Work, Family, and Community: A Framework for Fighting Poverty." *Annals of the American Academy of Political and Social Science* 686: 340–51.

Ray, Victor. 2019. "A Theory of Racialized Institutions." *American Sociological Review* 84 (1): 26–53.

Reese, Leslie. 2001. Morality and Identity in Mexican Immigrant Parents' Visions of the Future. *Journal of Ethnic and Migration Studies* 27: 455–72.

Reich, Jennifer A. 2005. *Fixing Families: Parents, Power, and the Child Welfare System*. New York: Routledge.

Rendon, Maria G. 2019. *Stagnant Dreamers: How the Inner City Shapes the Integration of the Second Generation*. New York: Russell Sage Foundation.

Rodgers-Dillon, Robin, and Lynne Haney. 2005. "Minimizing Vulnerability: Selective Interdependence after Welfare Reform." *Qualitative Sociology* 29(3): 235–54.

Sander, Richard, and Stuart Taylor Jr. 2012. *Mismatch: How Affirmative Action Hurts Students It's Intended to Help, and Why Universities Won't Admit It.* New York: Basic Books.

Schur, E. M., 1973. *Radical Nonintervention: Rethinking the Delinquency Problem.* Englewood Cliffs, NJ: Prentice-Hall.

Schwartz, Christine. 2013. "Trends and Variation in Assortative Mating: Causes and Consequences." *Annual Review of Sociology* 39: 451–70.

Schwarz, A. G., K. H. McVeigh, T. Matte, A. Goodman, D. Kass, and B. Kerker. 2008. "Childhood Asthma in New York City." *NYC Vital Signs* 7(1): 1–4.

Scott, Marvin, and Stanford Lyman. 1968. "Accounts." *American Sociological Review* 33: 46–62.

Seefeldt, Kristin. 2016. *Abandoned Families: Social Isolation in the 21st Century.* New York: Russell Sage Foundation.

Sered, Susan Starr, and Maureen Norton-Hawk. 2014. *Can't Catch a Break: Gender, Jail, Drugs and the Limits of Personal Responsibility.* Oakland: University of California Press.

Sharkey, Patrick. 2013. *Stuck in Place: Urban Neighborhoods and the End of Progress toward Racial Equality.* Chicago: University of Chicago Press.

Shim, Janet. 2010. "Cultural Health Capital: A Theoretical Approach to Understanding Health Care Interactions and the Dynamics of Unequal Treatment." *Journal of Health and Social Behavior* 51(1): 1–15.

Soss, Joe, Richard Fording, and Sanford Schram. 2011. *Disciplining the Poor: Neoliberal Paternalism and the Persistent Power of Race.* Chicago: University of Chicago Press.

Stack, Carol. 1974. *All Our Kin: Strategies for Survival in a Black Community.* New York: Basic Books.

Suarez-Orozco, M. 1989. *Central American Refugees and US High Schools: A Psychosocial Study of Motivation and Achievement.* Stanford, CA: Stanford University Press.

Sugie, Naomi. 2012. "Punishment and Welfare: Paternal Incarceration and Families' Receipt of Public Assistance." *Social Forces* 90(4): 1403–27.

Thorpe, Lorna E., Deborah G. List, Terry Marx, Linda May, Steven D. Helgerson, and Thomas R. Frieden. 2004. "Childhood Obesity in New York City Elementary School Students." *American Journal of Public Health* 94(9): 1496–500.

Tyler, Tom. 2006. *Why People Obey the Law: Procedural Justice, Legitimacy, and Compliance.* Princeton, NJ: Princeton University Press.

US Census Bureau. 2019. 2013–2017 American Community Survey 5-Year Estimates. Table S1701, "Poverty Status in the Past 12 Months." Retrieved from https://data.census.gov/cedsci/table?q=ACSST1Y2019.S1701&tid=ACSST1Y2019.S1701&hidePreview=true.

Wacquant, Loic. 2009. *Punishing the Poor: The Neoliberal Government of Social Insecurity.* Durham, NC: Duke University Press.

Wakefield, Sara, and Christopher Wildeman. 2013. *Children of the Prison Boom: Mass Incarceration and the Future of American Inequality.* New York: Oxford University Press.

Wallach, Jonathan B., and Mariano J. Rey. 2009. "A Socioeconomic Analysis of Obesity and Diabetes in New York City" *Preventing Chronic Disease* 6(3). Accessed on-line at http:/www.cdc.gov/pcd/issues/2009/jul/08_0215.htm.

Waller, Maureen. 2019. "Getting the Court in Your Business: Unmarried Parents, Institutional Intersectionality, and Establishing Parenting Time Orders in Family Court." *Social Problems* accessed online at https://doi.org/10.1093/socpro/spz029.

Waters, Mary C., Van C. Tran, Philip Kasinitz, and John H. Mollenkopf. 2010. "Segmented Assimilation Revisited: Types of Acculturation and Socioeconomic Outcomes in Young Adulthood." *Ethnic and Racial Studies* 33(7): 1168–93.

Watkins-Hayes, Celeste. 2009. *New Welfare Bureaucrats: Entanglements of Race, Class, and Policy Reform.* Chicago: University of Chicago Press.

Weber, Max. 1968. *Economy and Society.* Edited by Guenther Roth and Claus Wittich. New York: Bedminister. Originally: (1921) 1976.

Wildeman, Christopher, Sara Wakefield, and Hedwig Lee, eds. 2016. *Tough on Crime, Tough on Families? Criminal Justice and Family Life in America.* Special edition, *Annals of the American Academy of Political and Social Science.*

Index

Made in the USA
Middletown, DE
12 January 2023

21985281R00113